S V E N D   B R I N K M A N N

QUALITATIVE
INTERVIEWING

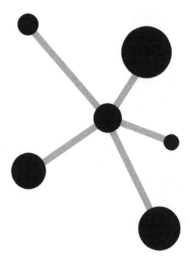

OXFORD
UNIVERSITY PRESS

OXFORD
UNIVERSITY PRESS

Oxford University Press is a department of the University of Oxford.
It furthers the University's objective of excellence in research, scholarship,
and education by publishing worldwide.

Oxford   New York
Auckland   Cape Town   Dar es Salaam   Hong Kong   Karachi
Kuala Lumpur   Madrid   Melbourne   Mexico City   Nairobi
New Delhi   Shanghai   Taipei   Toronto

With offices in
Argentina   Austria   Brazil   Chile   Czech Republic   France   Greece
Guatemala   Hungary   Italy   Japan   Poland   Portugal   Singapore
South Korea   Switzerland   Thailand   Turkey   Ukraine   Vietnam

Oxford is a registered trademark of Oxford University Press
in the UK and certain other countries.

Published in the United States of America by
Oxford University Press
198 Madison Avenue, New York, NY 10016

© Oxford University Press 2013

Library of Congress Cataloging-in-Publication Data
Brinkmann, Svend.
Qualitative interviewing / Svend Brinkmann.
   pages cm
Includes bibliographical references.
ISBN 978-0-19-986139-2
1. Interviewing.   2. Interviewing in sociology.   3. Qualitative research.   I. Title.
H61.28.B75 2013
001.4'33—dc23
2012047290

Printed in the United States of America
on acid-free paper

CONTENTS

PREFACE

The purpose of this book is to help readers write, represent, understand, and critique qualitative interview research as currently practiced. Its primary aim is not to tell readers how to conduct qualitative interviewing. Many other books exist for those who are interested in learning how to interview well for research purposes (e.g. Kvale & Brinkmann, 2008). Learning how to conduct interview research well does, however, rest on an acquaintance with the end product of the research process, viz. published articles and books that have used qualitative interviews. When acquiring the skills of interviewing, one should know what to aim for. In this regard, I hope the present book is useful for those who want to learn how to interview, even if it does not instruct them directly in doing so, because it describes and discusses a number of interview studies of high quality with an eye to how such studies have approached and communicated issues of research design, methodology, and research findings.

Overview of the Book

The book has four main chapters. The chapters build on each other to some extent, but they can also be read individually, depending on the reader's specific interests. The extensive introductory Chapter 1 gives an overview of the variegated landscape of qualitative interviewing. After recounting the history of interviewing in the social sciences, the chapter summarizes the central epistemological and theoretical positions on interviewing. Particular attention is given to the complementary positions of experience-focused interviewing (phenomenological positions) and language-focused interviewing (discourse oriented positions), which focus respectively on interview talk as *reports* (of the experiences of interviewees) and *accounts* (occasioned by the situation of interviewing).

Chapter 2 on research design maintains a focus on the two main positions and describes certain well-tested ways of designing interview studies. Four common steps in a research process are described: *preparation, interviewing, analysis,* and *reporting.* It is argued that different design questions arise from different interests in knowledge production, and interviews can be used in particular for purposes of discovery, construction, and understanding aspects of our social and personal worlds.

Chapter 3 is about how to write up the methodological procedures of an interview study. The most general rule across paradigmatic differences is: Describe what you have done and why. After describing the elements that commonly figure in interview reports (e.g. journal articles and dissertations), I present three ways of thinking about the methods section: as a prelude to presenting the analyses and findings, as a postscript to the text; and as embedded and integrated in the text. I also discuss how to deal with the fact that in qualitative interviewing, the researcher herself is the most important "instrument" for producing knowledge. A good methods section should address this "instrument," while other parts of the methods section can be more mechanical.

A common problem in qualitative interviewing concerns how to reduce or condense the often large amounts of data in interview studies. Chapter 4, on writing up the research findings, uses this problem as a springboard for describing more generally how to report research findings in ways that are both compelling and rigorous. The chapter refers to examples of findings that are based on theoretical readings of qualitative data, and also discusses ways of presenting findings that are much freer from social science theory. There are numerous ways of writing up the findings, among them ways that make use of inductive, deductive, and abductive strategies, which are all discussed. The chapter also advocates the use of displays, which are graphic presentations of large amounts of data in ways that include what is central and makes transparent what has been left out.

In the concluding Chapter 5, a number of the most common errors in interview reports are discussed, as are criticisms that have been raised against interview findings in recent years. A range of solutions are suggested to improve the quality of communication of research findings. The chapter also describes and discusses different strategies for evaluating research findings based on qualitative interviews. Recently, the question of quality criteria in qualitative inquiry has been much discussed, and some influential approaches are introduced and discussed. Again, the book distinguishes between traditional and more experimental perspectives on qualitative interviewing. Traditional perspectives will put emphasis on transparency, reliability, and possibly generalizability, whereas more experimental perspectives typically underline the aesthetic and moral implications of the research findings.

ACKNOWLEDGMENTS

A big thank you to Patricia Leavy, editor of the *Understanding Qualitative Research* book series, for getting in touch with me about this book project. Patricia has been helpful and very generous throughout the project. I was very grateful to be thought of as a potential author of a book on qualitative interviewing for this book series. Now that the book is done, I hope the result lives up to at least some of the expectations! I would also like to thank Abby Gross and Joanna Ng from Oxford University Press for facilitating a smooth process, and Rasmus Birk and Steffen Ernøe for having read the manuscript at a late stage from students' perspectives. When doing research for this book, I contacted a number of people about their favorite interview studies. I would like to thank Norman Denzin, Alexa Hepburn, Janice Morse, Martin Packer, Ian Parker, and Bettie St. Pierre for generously spending time preparing answers for me, and for allowing me to quote their answers in this book. I would also like to thank Aalborg University for allowing me to spend most of June 2012 in London, which gave me time to concentrate on this manuscript. Thanks also to Flora Cornish and Alex Gillespie for welcoming me and my family in London, and to the London School of Economics.

I dedicate this book to my children—Jens, Karl, and Ellen—who show me every day why conversations are endlessly fascinating and important in our lives. Thank you for all your words!

QUALITATIVE
INTERVIEWING

1

INTRODUCTION TO QUALITATIVE INTERVIEWING

QUALITATIVE INTERVIEWING has today become a key method in the human and social sciences, and also in many other corners of the scientific landscape such as education and the health sciences. Some have even argued that interviewing has become *the* central resource through which the social sciences—and society—engage with the issues that concern us (Rapley, 2001). For as long as we know, human beings have used conversation as a central tool to obtain knowledge about others. People talk with others in order to learn about how they experience the world, how they think, act, feel and develop as individuals and in groups, and in recent decades such knowledge-producing conversations have been refined and discussed as *interviews*.[1]

This chapter gives an overview of the landscape of qualitative interviewing. But what are interviews? In a classic text, Maccoby and Maccoby defined the interview as "a face-to-face verbal exchange, in which one person, the interviewer, attempts to elicit information or expressions of opinion or belief from

---

1. The first journalistic interviews appeared in the middle of the 19th century (Silvester, 1993), and social science interviews emerged in the course of the 20th century (see the history of interviewing recounted later in this chapter).

another person or persons." (Maccoby & Maccoby, 1954, p. 449). This definition can be used as a very general starting point, but we shall soon see that different schools of qualitative interviewing have interpreted, modified, and added to such a generic characterization in many different ways.

I begin this chapter by giving an introduction to the broader conversational world of human beings in which interviewing—as one specific kind of conversational practice—takes place. I then provide a brief history of qualitative interviewing before introducing a number of conceptual and analytical distinctions relevant to the central epistemological and theoretical questions in the field of qualitative interviewing. The chapter gives particular attention to the complementary positions of experience-focused interviewing (phenomenological positions) and language-focused interviewing (discourse oriented positions). These—together with another distinction between traditional and more experimental ways of designing and writing-up interview studies—are intended to structure the arguments and examples throughout the book chapters,

Qualitative interviewing in a conversational world

Human beings are conversational creatures that live a dialogical life (Mulhall, 2007). Humankind is, in the words of philosopher Stephen Mulhall, "a kind of enacted conversation." (Mulhall, 2007, p. 58). From the earliest days of our lives, we are able to enter into proto-conversations with caregivers in ways that involve subtle forms of turn-taking and emotional communication. The pairings in which our earliest conversations occur are known to be prior to the child's own sense of self. We are therefore communicating, and indeed conversational, creatures before we become subjective and monological ones (Trevarthen, 1993).

Of course, most of us do learn to talk privately to ourselves, and hide our emotional lives from others, but this is possible only because there was first an intersubjective communicative process with others. Our relationships with others—and also with ourselves—are thus conversational. In order to understand ourselves, we must use a language that was first acquired conversationally, and we try out our interpretations in dialogue with others and the world. The human self exists only within what philosopher Charles Taylor has called "webs of interlocution" (Taylor, 1989, p. 36).

Our very inquiring and interpreting selves are conversational at their core; they are constituted by the numerous relationships we have, and have had, with other people (Brinkmann, 2012a).

Unsurprisingly, conversations are therefore a rich and indispensable source of knowledge about personal and social aspects of our lives. In a philosophical sense, all human research is conversational, since we are linguistic creatures and language is best understood in the context of conversation (Mulhall, 2007). Since the late 19th century (in journalism) and the early 20th century (in the social sciences), the conversational process of knowing has been conceptualized under the name of *interviewing*. The very term interview itself testifies to the dialogical and interactional nature of human life. An interview is literally an *inter-view*, an interchange of views between two persons, conversing about a subject of mutual interest (Kvale & Brinkmann, 2008). *Con-versation* in its Latin root means "dwelling with someone" or "wandering together with," and the root sense of *dia-logue* is that of talk (*logos*) that goes back and forth (*dia-*) between persons (Mannheim & Tedlock, 1995, p. 4).

Thus conceived, the concept of conversation in the human and social sciences should be thought of as much broader than simply another specific and technical research method. Certainly, conversations in the form of interviewing have been refined into a set of techniques—to be explicated throughout this book—but they are also a mode of knowing and a fundamental ontology of persons. As philosopher Rom Harré has put it: "The primary human reality is persons in conversation." (Harré, 1983, p. 58). Cultures are constantly produced, reproduced, and revised in dialogues among their members (Mannheim & Tedlock, 1995, p. 2).

Our everyday lives are thus conversational to their core. This also goes for the investigation of cultural phenomena, or what we call social science. We should see language, culture, and human self-understanding as emergent properties of conversations rather than the other way around. Dialogues are not several monologues that are added together, but the basic, primordial form of associated human life. In John Shotter's words:

[W]e live our daily social lives within an ambience of conversation, discussion, argumentation, negotiation, criticism and justification; much of it to do with problems of intelligibility and the legitimation of claims to truth. (Shotter, 1993, p. 29).

The pervasiveness of conversation in human life is both a burden and a blessing for qualitative interviewers. On the one hand, qualitative interviewing appears as a very significant tool with which to understand central features of our conversational world. Contrary to widespread criticisms that qualitative research is too subjective, one might argue—given the picture of the conversational reality painted here—that qualitative interviewing is in fact the most *objective* method of inquiry when one is interested in qualitative features of human experience, talk, and interaction (at least if objectivity means being adequate to a subject matter). Qualitative interviews seem uniquely capable of grasping these features of our lives.

On the other hand, it is also a burden for qualitative interviewers that they use conversations to study a world, which is always already itself saturated with conversation. If Mulhall is right that humankind is a kind of enacted conversation, then the process of studying humans by the use of interviewing is analogous to fish wanting to study water. Fish surely "know" what water is in a practical, embodied sense, but it can be a great challenge to see and understand the obvious, that with which we are so familiar (Brinkmann, 2012a).

Similarly, some interview researchers might think that interviewing others for research purposes is easy and simple to do, because it employs a set of techniques that everyone masters by virtue of being capable of asking questions and recording the answers. This, however, is clearly an illusory simplicity, and many qualitative interviewers, even experienced ones, will recognize the frustrating experience of having conducted a large number of interviews (which is often the most fun part of a research project), but ending up with a huge amount of data, in the form of perhaps hundreds or even thousands of pages of transcripts, and not knowing how to transform this material into a solid, relevant, and thought-provoking analysis. Too much time is often spent on interviewing, while too little time is devoted to preparing for the interviews, and subsequently to analyzing the empirical materials. And, to continue on this note, too little time is normally used to reflect on the role of interviewing as a knowledge-producing social practice in itself. Interviewing, in short, is often simply taken for granted.

A further burden for today's qualitative interviewers concerns the fact that interviewees are often almost too familiar with their role in the conversation. As Atkinson and Silverman argued some years ago, we live in an *interview society*, where the self is continually produced in confessional settings ranging from talk shows to research interviews (Atkinson & Silverman, 1997). As most of us, at least in the imagined hemisphere we call the West, are acquainted with interviews and their more or less standardized choreographies, qualitative interviews sometimes become a rather easy and regular affair, with few breaks and cracks in conventions and norms, even though such breaks and cracks are often the most interesting aspects of conversational episodes (Roulston, 2010; Tanggaard, 2007).

On the side of interviewers, Atkinson and Silverman find that "in promoting a particular view of narratives of personal experience, researchers too often recapitulate, in an uncritical fashion, features of the contemporary interview society" where "the interview becomes a personal confessional" (Atkinson & Silverman, 1997, p. 305). Although conversation in a broad sense is a human universal, qualitative interviewers often forget that the social practice of research interviewing in a narrower sense is a historically and culturally specific mode of interacting, and they too often construe "face-to-face interaction" as "the primordial, natural setting for communication," as anthropologist Charles Briggs has pointed out (Briggs, 2007, p. 554).

As a consequence, the analysis of interviews is generally limited to what takes place during the concrete interaction phase with its questions and responses. In contrast to this, a recurring theme of this book will be that excellent interview research does not just communicate a number of answers to the interviewer's questions, with the interviewer's interpretive interjections added on, but includes an analytic focus on what Briggs has called "the larger set of practices of knowledge production that makes up the research from beginning to end" (Briggs, 2007, p. 566). Just as it is crucial in quantitative and experimental research to have an adequate understanding of the technologies of experimentation, it is crucial in qualitative interviewing to understand the intricacies of this quite specific knowledge-producing practice. Interviewers should be particularly careful not to take for granted the form of human relationship that is a qualitative research interview and simply gloss it over as an unproblematic, direct, and universal source of knowledge.

The History of Qualitative Interviewing

This takes us directly to the history of qualitative interviewing, for only by tracking the history of how our current practices came to be can we fully understand their contingent natures and reflect on their roles in how we produce conversational knowledge today.

In one obvious sense, the use of conversations for knowledge-producing purposes is likely as old as human language and communication. The fact that we can pose questions to others concerning things about which we are unknowledgeable is a core capability of the human species. It expands our intellectual powers enormously, since it enables us to share and distribute knowledge among us. Without this fundamental capability, it would be hard to imagine what human life would be like. It is furthermore a capacity that has developed into many different forms and ramifications in human societies. Emory Bogardus, an early American sociologist and founder of one of the first U.S. sociology departments (at the University of Southern California) declared in 1924 that interviewing "is as old as the human race" (Bogardus, 1924, p. 456), and he discussed similarities and differences between the ways that physicians, lawyers, priests, journalists, detectives, social workers, and psychiatrists conduct interviews with a remarkable sensitivity to the details of such different conversational practices.

In a more specific sense, and more essentially related to qualitative interviewing as a scientific human enterprise, conversations were used by Thucydides in ancient Greece as he interviewed participants from the Peloponnesian Wars to write the history of the wars. At roughly the same time, Socrates famously questioned—or we might even say *interviewed*—his fellow citizens in ancient Athens and used the dialogues to develop knowledge about perennial human questions related to justice, truth, beauty, and the virtues. In recent years, some interview scholars have sought to rehabilitate a Socratic practice of interviewing, not least as an alternative to the often long monologues of phenomenological and narrative approaches to interviewing and in an attempt to think of interviews as practices that can create a knowledgeable citizenry and not merely chart common opinions and attitudes (see Dinkins, 2005, who unites Socrates with a hermeneutic approach to dialogical knowledge and Brinkmann, 2007a). Such varieties of interviewing have come to be known as dialogic and confrontational (Roulston, 2010, p. 26), although care should be taken not to understand the latter term as implying some disrespectful practice of catching the interviewee in contradictions or something like that. I return to active, dialogic, and confrontational interview formats below.

If we jump to more recent times, interviewing notably entered the human sciences with the advent of Sigmund Freud's psychoanalysis around 1900. Freud is famous for his psychoanalytic theory of the unconscious, but it is significant that he developed this revolutionary theory (which, in many ways, changed the Western conception of humanity) through therapeutic conversations, or what he referred to as the talking cure. Freud conducted several hundred interviews with patients that used the patients' free associations as a conversational engine. The therapist/interviewer should display what Freud called an "evenly-hovering attention" and be alert to anything that emerges as important (Freud, 1963). Freud made clear that research and treatment go hand in hand in psychoanalysis, and Steinar Kvale has more recently pointed to the rich potentials of psychoanalytic conversations for qualitative interviewing even today (Kvale, 2003).

Others have re-actualized psychoanalysis in other ways. Wendy Hollway and Tony Jefferson have developed a specific notion of the interview that is based on the psychoanalytic idea of "the defended subject" (Hollway & Jefferson, 2000). In their eyes, interviewees "are motivated *not* to know certain aspects of themselves and...they *produce* biographical accounts which avoid such knowledge." (p. 169). This, obviously, has implications for how interviewers should proceed with analysis and interpretation of biographical statements of interviewees and is a quite different approach to interviewing compared to more humanistic forms, as we shall see.

Although psychoanalysis has been relegated to the periphery of psychology and psychiatry in recent years, it has survived in departments of literature and cultural studies, and discursive psychologists still provide fruitful readings of psychoanalytic theory that reinterpret the unconscious as a social and discursive mechanism; see in particular Michael Billig's *Freudian Repression* with a subtitle that is relevant in the present context: "Conversation creating the unconscious" (Billig, 1999).

Many human and social scientists in the first half of the 20th century, including those who pioneered in qualitative interviewing, were well versed in psychoanalytic theory. Jean Piaget, the famous developmental researcher, had even received training as a psycho-analyst, but his approach to interviewing is worth mentioning in its own right. Piaget's (1930) theory of child development was based on his interviews with children (often his own) in natural settings, frequently in combination with different experimental tasks. He would typically let the children talk freely about the weight and size of objects, or, in relation to his research on moral development, about different moral problems (Piaget, 1932), and he would take notice of the manner in which their thoughts unfolded.

Raymond Lee, one of the few historians of interviewing, has charted how Piaget's so-called "clinical" method of interviewing became an inspiration for Elton Mayo, who was responsible for one of the largest interview studies in history at the Hawthorne plant in Chicago in the 1920s (Lee, 2011). This study arose from a need to interpret the curious results of a number of practical experiments on the effects of changes in illumination on production at the plant: It seemed that work output improved when the lighting of the production rooms was increased, but also when it was decreased. This instigated a study in which more than 21,000 workers were interviewed for more than an hour each. The study was reported by Roethlisberger & Dickson (1939), but Mayo laid out the method-ological procedures, including careful—and surprisingly contem-porary—advice to interviewers that is worth quoting at length:

1. Give your whole attention to the person interviewed, and make it evident that you are doing so.
2. Listen—don't talk.
3. Never argue; never give advice.
4. Listen to:
   (a) what he wants to say
   (b) what he does not want to say
   (c) what he cannot say without help
5. As you listen, plot out tentatively and for subsequent cor-rection the pattern (personal) that is being set before you. To test this, from time to time summarize what has been said and present for comment (e.g. "is this what you are telling me?"). Always do this with the greatest caution, that is, clarify in ways that do not add or distort.
6. Remember that everything said must be considered a personal confidence and not divulged to anyone. (Mayo, 1933, p. 65).

Many approaches to, and textbooks on, interviewing still follow such guidelines today, often forgetting, however, the specific historical circumstances under which this practice emerged.

Not just Piaget, but also the humanistic psychologist Carl Rogers, was an important psychological pioneer of interviewing. Like Freud, Rogers developed a conversational technique that was useful both in therapeutic contexts (so-called client-centered therapy), and in research interviews, which he referred to as the "non-directive method as a technique for social research" (Rogers, 1945). As he explained, the goal of this kind of therapy/research was to sample the respondent's attitudes toward herself: "Through the non-directive interview we have an unbiased method by which we may plumb these private thoughts and perceptions of the individual." (p. 282). In contrast to psychoanalytic practice, the respondent in client-centered therapy/research is a client rather than a patient, and the client is the expert (and hardly a "defended subject"). Although often framed in different terms, many contemporary interview researchers still conceptualize the research interview in line with Rogers' humanistic, non-directive approach, putting emphasis on the respondents' private experiences, narratives, opinions, beliefs, and attitudes.

As Lee recounts, the methods of interviewing developed at the Hawthorne plant in the 1930s aroused interest among sociologists at the University of Chicago, who made it part of their methodological repertoire (Lee, 2011, p. 132). Rogers himself moved to Chicago in 1945 and was involved in interdisciplinary projects there. As is well known, the so-called Chicago School of sociology was highly influential in using and promoting a range of qualitative methods, not least ethnography, and it also spawned some of the most innovative theoretical developments in the social sciences, such as symbolic interactionism (e.g. Blumer, 1969).

As the Rogerian nondirective approach to interviewing gained in popularity, early critiques of this technique also emerged. In the 1950s, the famous sociologist David Riesman and his colleague Mark Benney criticized it for its lack of interviewer involvement, and they warned against the tendency to use the level of "rapport" (much emphasized by interviewers inspired by therapy) in an interview to judge the qualities of the interview concerning knowledge. They thought it was a prejudice "to assume the more rapport-filled and intimate the relation, the more 'truth' the respondent will vouchsafe"

(Riesman & Benney, 1956, p. 10). In their eyes, rapport-filled interviews often spill over with "the flow of legend and cliché" (p. 11), since interviewees are likely to adapt their responses to what they think the interviewer expects from them (see also Lee, 2008, for an account of Riesman's discussion of interviewing and its relevance even today). As we shall see in this book, issues such as these, which were raised more than 50 years ago, continue to be pertinent and largely unresolved in today's interview research. The mid-20th century witnessed a number of other large interview studies that remain classics in the field, but which have also shaped public opinion about different issues. I shall mention three of these that dealt with topics such as authoritarianism, sexuality, and consumer behavior.

After the Second World War, there was a pressing need to understand the roots of anti-Semitism, and *The Authoritarian Personality*, by the well-known critical theorist Adorno and co-workers, controversially traced these roots to an authoritarian upbringing (Adorno, Frenkel-Brunswik, Levinson & Sanford, 1950). Their study was based on interviews and employed a combination of open qualitative interviews and much more structured questionnaires to produce data. Although important knowledge of societal value may have been produced, the study has nonetheless been criticized on ethical grounds for using therapeutic techniques to get around the defenses of the interviewees in order to learn about their prejudices and authoritarian personality traits (Kvale & Brinkmann, 2008, p. 313).

Another famous interview study from the same period was Kinsey's *Sexual Behavior in the Human Male* (Kinsey, Pomeroy & Martin, 1948). The research group interviewed about 6,000 men for an hour or more about their sexual behaviors, which generated results that were shocking to the public. In addition to the fascinating results, the book contains many interesting reflections on interviewing, and the authors discuss in great detail how to put the interviewees at ease, how to assure privacy, and how to frame the sequencing of sensitive topics (the contributions of Adorno and Kinsey are also described in Platt, 2002). As Kinsey put it in the book:

> The interview has become an opportunity for him [the participant] to develop his own thinking, to express to himself his disappointments and hopes, to bring into the open things

that he has previously been afraid to admit to himself, to work out solutions to his difficulties. He quickly comes to realize that a full and complete confession will serve his own interests. (Kinsey, Pomeroy & Martin, 1948, p. 42).

The 2004 movie *Kinsey*, starring Liam Neeson, is worth seeing from an interviewer's point of view, since it shows these early interviewers in action.

It should also be mentioned that qualitative interviewing quickly entered market research in the course of the 20th century, which is hardly surprising as a consumer society developed in this period (Brinkmann & Kvale, 2005). A pioneer was Ernest Dichter, whose *The Strategy of Desire* (1960) communicates the results of an interview study about consumer motivation for buying a car. Interestingly, Dichter describes his interview technique as a "depth interview," inspired both by psychoanalysis and by the nondirective approach of Rogers. Market and consumer research continue to be among the largest areas of qualitative interviewing in contemporary consumer society, particularly in the form of focus groups. According to one estimate, as many as 5 percent of all adults in Great Britain have taken part in focus groups for marketing purposes, which certainly lends very concrete support to the thesis that we live in an "interview society" (Brinkmann & Kvale, 2005).

Along with the different empirical studies, we have also seen that academics in the Western world have produced an enormous number of books on qualitative interviewing as a method, both in the form of "how to" books, and in the form of more theoretical discussions. Spradley's *The Ethnographic Interview* (1979) and Mishler's *Research Interviewing: Context and Narrative* (1986) were two important early books—the former being full of concrete advice about how to ask questions, etc., and the latter being a thorough theoretical analysis of interviews as speech events involving a joint construction of meaning.

Following from the postmodern philosophies of social science that emerged in the early 1980s (e.g. Clifford & Marcus, 1986; Denzin, 1997; Lyotard, 1984), there has in the last couple of decades been a veritable and creative explosion in the kinds of interviews offered to researchers (see Fontana & Prokos, 2007). Many of these question both the psychoanalytic idea that it is possible to dig out truths from the psyche of the interviewee and the humanistic idea of the nondirective approach that interviews can be "an unbiased method," as Rogers had originally conceived it.

Roulston (2010) makes a comprehensive list of some of the most recent postmodern varieties of interviewing and also of more traditional ones (I have here shortened and adapted Roulston's longer list):

- *Neo-positivist* conceptions of the interview are still widespread and emphasize how the conversation can be used to reveal "the true self" of the interviewee (or the essence of her experiences), resulting in solid, trustworthy data that are only accessible through interviews with the interviewer having a noninterfering role.
- *Romantic* conceptions stress that the goal of interviewing is to obtain revelations and confessions of the interviewees by intimacy and rapport. These conceptions are somewhat close to neo-positivist ones, but put much more weight on the interviewer as an active and authentic midwife facilitating the "birth" of the inner psyche of the interviewee.
- *Constructionist* conceptions reject the romantic idea of authenticity and favor an idea of a subject that is locally produced *in* the situation. There is thus a focus on the situational practice of interviewing and a distrust toward discourses of data as permanent "nuggets" to be "mined" by the interviewer. Instead, the interviewer is often portrayed as a "traveler," involved in the co-construction of whatever happens in the conversation together with the interviewee (Kvale & Brinkmann, 2008).
- *Postmodern* and *transformative* conceptions stage interviews as dialogic and performative events that aim to bring new kinds of people and new worlds into being. The interview is depicted as a chance for people to get together and create new possibilities for action. Some transformative conceptions focus on potential decolonizing aspects of interviewing, seeking to subvert the colonizing tendencies that some see in standard interviewing (Smith, 1999). In addition, we can mention feminist (Reinharz & Chase, 2002) and collaborative forms of interviewing (Ellis & Berger, 2003) that aim for an engaged practice of interviewing that focuses more on the

INTRODUCTION TO QUALITATIVE INTERVIEWING : 13

researchers' experience than standard procedures, sometimes expressed through autoethnography, an approach
that seeks to unite ethnographical and autobiographical
intentions (Ellis, Adams & Bochner, 2011).

It goes without saying that the overarching line of historical development laid out here, beginning in the earliest years of
recorded human history and ending with postmodern, transformative, and co-constructed interviewing, is highly selective, and it
could have been presented in countless different ways. I have made
no attempt to divide the history of qualitative interviewing into
historical phases; I believe this would obscure the criss-crossing of
lines of inspiration from different knowledge-producing practices
through conversations. Socrates as an active interviewer inspires
some of today's constructionist and postmodern interviewers,
while Freud and Rogers as clinical interviewers became important to people who use interviewing for purposes related to marketing and industry. It seems that the only general rule is that no
approach is ever completely left behind, but that everything can
be—and often is—recycled in new clothing. This should not surprise us, since the richness and historical variability of the human
conversational world demand that researchers use different conversational means of knowledge production.

In light of the centrality of qualitative interviewing in the academic world, and also more generally in the "interview society,"
it is surprising to observe the scarcity of historical studies of the
emergence and development of this conversational practice.
Nevertheless, we shall now leave the historical line of development, but later in the chapter, I return to some of the historical
examples and place them in a heuristic taxonomy of approaches to
interviewing in order to sum up and give an overview of the many
different varieties. Before moving on, however, I will introduce
an example of what a typical qualitative interview may look like,
taken from my own research, to illustrate what all this is about.

An Example of Qualitative Interviewing

The following excerpt is from an interview I conducted about
10 years ago. It was part of a research project in which I studied ethical dilemmas and moral reasoning in psychotherapeutic

practice. The project was exploratory and sought an understanding of clinical psychologists' own experiences with ethical problems in their work. The excerpt in Box 1.1 does not represent an ideal interview, but it illustrates a common choreography inherent in much qualitative interviewing.

Box 1.1 An Interview on Ethics and Psychotherapy

At the time of the interview, the interviewee was in her early 50s and had been a practicing psychologist for about 25 years. The interview was conducted in Danish, and I have translated it into English myself.

After some introductory remarks and an initial briefing, I, the interviewer (SB), go straight to a question that I had prepared in advance and ask the interviewee (IE) for a description of a concrete ethical dilemma (the numbers in square brackets refer to elements of the conversation that are addressed below):

SB: [1] First I'd like to ask you to think back and describe a situation from your work as a psychologist in which you experienced an ethical dilemma...or a situation that in some way demanded special ethical considerations from you.

IE: [2] Actually, I believe I experience those all the time. Well...I believe that the very fact that therapeutic work with other people demands that you keep...I don't know if it is a dilemma—that's what you asked about, right?—well, I don't know if it's a dilemma, but I think I have ethical considerations all the time. Considerations about how best to treat this human being with respect are demanded all the time...with the respect that is required, and I believe that there are many ethical considerations there. Ahm...When you work therapeutically you become very personal, get very close to another human being, and I think that is something you have to bear in mind constantly: How far are you allowed to go? How much can you enter into someone else's universe? But that is not a dilemma, is it?

SB: I guess it can be. Can you think of a concrete situation in which you faced this question about how close you can go, for example?

IE: [3] Yes, I can. I just had a ...a woman, whose husband has a mental disorder, or he has had a severe personality disorder, so their family life is much affected by this. And she comes to me to process this situation of hers, having two small children and a husband, and a system of treatment, which sometimes helps out and sometimes doesn't. And it is very difficult for her to accept that someone close to her has a mental disorder or is fragile, it's actually a long process. She is a nurse and family life has more or less been idyllic before he ...before the personality disorder really emerged. So it is extremely difficult for her to accept that this family, which she had imagined would be the place for her children to grow up, is not going to be like that. It is actually going to be very, very different. And she tries to fight it all the time: "It just *might* be ...if only ...I guess it will be ..." And it is *never* going to be any different! And there lies a dilemma, I think: How much is it going to be: "This is something you *have* to face, it is *never* going to be different!" So I have to work to make her pose the question herself: "What do you think? How long time ...What are your thoughts? Do you think it will be different? What do they tell you at the psychiatric hospital? What is your experience?" And right now she is getting closer to seeing ...I might fear that it ends in a divorce; I am not sure that she can cope with it. But no one can know this. I think there is a dilemma here, or some considerations about how much to push and press forward.

SB: [4] Yes, the dilemma is perhaps that you—with your experience and knowledge about these matters—can see that the situation is not going to change much from its current state?

IE: It certainly won't.

SB: And the question is ...

IE: ...how much I should push, for she does actually know this intellectually. [5] We have talked about it lots of times. But emotionally she hasn't ...she doesn't have the power to face it. One day I told her: "I don't think you develop, I don't think anything happens to you, before you accept emotionally that he is not going to change." I put her on the spot and she kept evading it and so on, but it ... "You don't accept it; I can tell that you don't accept it. You understand it intellectually, but you still hope that it passes." I pushed her a lot then. But I don't know if this is an ethical dilemma, I am not sure ...

These few exchanges of questions and answers follow a certain conversational flow that is common in qualitative interviews that can be divided into [1] *question*; [2] *negotiation of meaning* concerning questions and themes, including clarification; [3] *concrete description* from the interviewee; [4] the interviewer's *interpretation* of the description; [5] *coda* (and then the cycle can start over with a new question, or else—as in this case—further questions about the same description can be posed).

The sequence begins when I pose a question, [1], that calls for a concrete description; a question that seems to make sense to the interviewee. However, she cannot immediately think of, or articulate, an episode that illustrates what comes to her mind, and she is in doubt concerning the meaning of one of the central concepts in the opening question (an "ethical dilemma"). This happens very often, and it can be quite difficult for interviewees (as for all of us) to describe concretely what one has experienced instead of speaking in general terms (especially for professionals who have many general scripts at their disposal). There is some negotiation and attunement between us [2], before she decides to talk about a specific situation, but even though this is interesting and well described by the interviewee [3], she ends by returning (in what I call the coda) to a doubt about the appropriateness of the example. Before this, I summarize and rephrase her description [4], which she validates, before she herself provides a kind of evaluation in the coda [5]. After this, I have a number of follow-up questions that ask the interviewee to tell more about the situation, before a new question is introduced, and a similar conversational flow is followed again.

The uncertainty of the interviewee about her own example around [2] illustrates the importance of assuring the interviewee that he or she is the expert concerning personal experience. The interviewer should make clear that generally there are no right or wrong answers or examples in qualitative interviewing, and that the interviewer is interested in anything the interviewee comes up with. It is very common to find that participants are eager to be "good interviewees," wanting to give the researcher something that is valuable, and this can paradoxically block the production of interesting stories and descriptions (although it did not in the present case).

In this case, a key point of the study became the term "ethical dilemma" itself, a term that is currently a nodal point in a huge number of different discourses with many different meanings, and it was thus interesting to hear different respondents' immediate understandings of the term. Their widespread uncertainty concerning the referents of the term (which was shared by the interviewer!) was not only understandable, but actually conducive to developing my ideas further about (professional) ethics as something occurring in a zone of doubt rather than certainty (as otherwise stressed by some procedural approaches to ethics).

When I first set out to conduct this study, I had something like a neo-positivist conception of interviewing in mind, in Roulston's sense, believing that there were certain essential features connected to the experience of ethically difficult situations. When working further with the theme, and after learning from my interviewees, I gradually grew suspicious of this idea, and I also came to appreciate a more constructionist conception of interviewing, according to which the interview situation itself—which includes the interviewer—plays an important role in the production of talk.

Other things to note at this stage include the asymmetrical distribution of talk that can be observed between the two conversationalists: The interviewer poses rather short questions, and the interviewee gives long and elaborated answers. This is not always so (some respondents are more reluctant or simply less talkative), but this asymmetry has been highlighted as a sign of quality in the literature on qualitative interviewing (e.g. Kvale & Brinkmann, 2008). In general, as readers of interview reports we would like to hear what the interviewees have to say rather than listening to the researcher. There is also quite a bit of dramatization in the interviewee's talk in the excerpt, i.e. when she uses reported speech to stage a dialogue between herself and her client, which signals that she is capable with words and a good story teller. On the side of the interviewer, we see that no attempts are made to contradict or question the interviewee's account, and the part of the interview that is quoted here thus looks quite a bit like what was recommended by Mayo and later non-directive interviewers: The interviewer listens a lot and does not talk much, he does not argue or give advice, and he plots out tentatively (in [4]) what the interviewee is saying, which is commented upon and verified by the interviewee (cf. Mayo, 1933, p. 65).

Different Forms of Qualitative Research Interviews

The semi-structured, face-to-face interview in the example is quite typical, but it merely represents one form an interview may take, and there is today a huge variety of other forms. Each form has certain advantages and disadvantages that researchers and recipients of research alike should be aware of. I shall here describe how qualitative interviews may differ in terms of *structure*, the *number of participants* in each interview, different *media*, and also different *interviewer styles*. After this I will go on to look at two broad ways of theorizing interview talk that will be a recurrent theme throughout this book.

Structure

It is quite common to make a distinction between structured, semi-structured, and unstructured interviews. This distinction, however, should be thought of as a continuum ranging from relatively structured to relatively unstructured formats. I use the word "relatively," because, on the one end of the continuum, as Parker (2005) argues, there really is no such thing as a completely structured interview "because people always say things that spill beyond the structure, before the interview starts and when the recorder has been turned off." (p. 53). Utterances that "spill beyond the structure" are often quite important, and are even sometimes the key to understanding the interviewee's answers to the pre-structured questions. One line of criticism against standardized survey interviewing actually concerns the fact that meanings and interpretive frames that go beyond the predetermined structure are left out, with the risk that the researcher cannot understand what actually goes on in the interaction.

We might add to Parker's argument that there is also no such thing as a completely *unstructured* interview, since the interviewer always has an idea about what should take place in the conversation. Even some of the least structured interviews such as life history interviews that only have one question prepared in advance (e.g. "I would like you to tell me the story of your life. Please begin as far back as you can remember and include as many details as possible") provide structure to the conversation by framing it in accordance with certain specific conversational norms rather than others. Another way to put the matter is to say that there are no such things as non-leading questions. All questions lead the interviewee in certain directions, but it is generally preferable to lead participants only to talk about certain *themes*, rather than to specific *opinions* about these themes.

So, it is not possible to avoid structure, nor would it be desirable, but it is possible to provide a structure that it flexible enough for interviewees to be able to raise questions and concerns in their own words and from their own perspectives. Anthropologist Bruno Latour has argued that this is one definition of objectivity that human and social science can work with in the sense of "allowing the object to object" (Latour, 2000). Latour pinpoints a problem in the human and social sciences related to the fact that for these sciences, and unlike the natural sciences: "Nothing is more difficult than to find a way to render objects able to object to the utterances that we make about them" (p. 115). He finds that human beings behave too easily as if they had been mastered by the researcher's agenda, which often results in trivial and predictable research that tells us nothing new (see in particular Latour, 1997). What should be done instead, according to Latour, is to allow research participants to be "interested, active, disobedient, fully involved in what is said about themselves by others" (Latour, 2000, p. 116). This does not imply a total elimination of structure, but demands a careful preparation and reflection of how to involve interviewees actively, how to avoid flooding the conversation with social science categories, and how to provoke interviewees respectfully to bring contrasting perspectives to light (Parker, 2005, p. 63). I shall return to this issue below when considering actively confronting interviewer styles.

In spite of this caveat—that neither completely structured nor completely unstructured interviews are possible—it may still be worthwhile to distinguish between more or less structure, with semi-structured interviews somewhere in the middle as the standard approach to qualitative interviewing.

- *Structured interviews*: These are employed in surveys and are typically based on the same research logic as questionnaires: Standardized ways of asking questions are thought to lead to answers that can be compared across participants and possibly quantified. Interviewers are supposed to "read questions exactly as worded to every respondent and are trained never to provide information beyond what is scripted in the questionnaire." (Conrad & Schober, 2008, p. 173). Although structured interviews are useful for some purposes, they do not take advantage of the dialogical potentials for knowledge production that are inherent in human conversations. They are passive recordings of people's opinions and attitudes, and often reveal more about the cultural conventions of how one should answer specific questions than about the conversational production of social life itself. Since this book is concerned with qualitative interviewing, which characteristically has as a much more flexible format with the interviewer being able to follow up freely on interviewee answers, I shall leave the standardized and structured interview format behind and refer the interested reader to the text by Conrad and Schober, who do in fact discuss creative ways of developing this traditional social science technique further (Conrad & Schober, 2008).

• *Unstructured interviews*: At the other end of the continuum lie interviews that have little preset structure. These are for example the life story interview seeking to highlight "the most important influences, experiences, circumstances, issues, themes, and lessons of a lifetime." (Atkinson, 2002, p. 125). What these are for an individual can only be known in the course of spending time with the interviewee, which means that the interviewer cannot prepare for a life story interview by devising a lot of specific questions, but must instead think about how to facilitate the telling of the life story. After the opening request for a narrative, the main role of the interviewer is to remain a listener, withholding desires to interrupt and sporadically asking questions that may clarify the story. The life story interview is a variant of the more general genre of narrative interviewing about which Wengraf's (2001) *Qualitative Research Interviewing* gives a particularly thorough account, focusing on biographical-narrative depth-interviews. These need not concern the life story as a whole, but may address other, more specific, storied aspects of human lives, building on the insight of narratology that human beings experience and act in the world through narratives. Narratives, in this light, are a root metaphor for psychological processes (Sarbin, 1986). With the more focused narrative interviews we get nearer to semi-structured interviews as the middle ground between structured and unstructured interviews.

- *Semi-structured interviews*: Interviews in the semi-structured format are sometimes equated with qualitative interviewing as such (Warren, 2002). They are probably also the most widespread ones in the human and social sciences and are sometimes the only format given attention in textbooks on qualitative research (e.g. Flick, 2002). For that reason, it is the format to which most of the focus of the present book will be devoted. Compared to structured interviews, semi-structured interviews can make better use of the knowledge-producing potentials of dialogues by allowing much more leeway for following up on whatever angles are deemed important by the interviewee. Semi-structured interviews also give the interviewer a greater chance of becoming visible as a knowledge-producing participant in the process itself, rather than hiding behind a preset interview guide. And, compared to unstructured interviews, the interviewer has a greater saying in focusing the conversation on issues that he or she deems important in relation to the research project.

One definition of the semi-structured qualitative research interview reads: "It is defined as an interview with the purpose of obtaining descriptions of the life world of the interviewee in order to interpret the meaning of the described phenomena." (Kvale & Brinkmann, 2008, p. 3). The key words here are (1) purpose, (2) descriptions, (3) life world, and (4) interpretation of meaning, which I shall now unfold in turn:

(1) *Purpose*: Unlike everyday conversations with friends or family members, qualitative interviews are not conducted for their own sake; they are not a goal in themselves, but are staged and conducted in order to serve the researcher's goal of producing knowledge (and there may be other, ulterior goals like obtaining a degree, furthering one's career, or positioning oneself in the field, etc.). All sorts of motives may play a role in the staging of interviews, and good interview reports often contain a *reflexive* account and discussion of both individual and social aspects of such motives (does it matter, for example, if the interviewer is a woman, perhaps identifying as a feminist, interviewing other women?). Clearly, the fact that interviews are conversations conducted for a purpose, which sets the agenda, raises a number of issues having to do with power and control that are important to reflect upon for epistemic reasons as well as for ethical ones (Brinkmann, 2007b).

(2) *Descriptions*: In most interview studies, the goal is to obtain the interviewee's descriptions rather than reflections or theorizations. In line with a widespread phenomenological perspective (to be explained more fully below), interviewers are normally seeking descriptions of *how* interviewees experience the world, its episodes and events, rather than speculations about *why* they have certain experiences. Good interview questions thus invite interviewees to give descriptions, such as "Could you please describe a situation for me in which you became angry?"; "What happened?"; "How did you experience anger?"; "How did it feel?" (Of course, only one of these questions should be posed at a time.) Good interviewers tend to avoid more abstract and reflective questions such as "What does anger mean to you?"; "If I say 'anger,' what do you think of then?"; "Why do you think that you tend to feel angry?" Such questions *may* be productive in the conversation, but interviewers will normally defer them until more descriptive aspects have been covered.

(3) *Life world*: The concept of the life world goes back to the founder of phenomenology, Edmund Husserl, who introduced it in 1936 in his book *The Crisis of the European Sciences* to refer to the intersubjectively shared and meaningful world in which humans conduct their lives and experience significant phenomena (Husserl, 1954). It is a pre-reflective and pre-theorized world in which anger, for example, is a meaningful human expression in response to having one's rights violated (or something similar) before it is a process occurring in the neurophysiological and endocrinological systems (and "before" should here be taken in a logical, rather than temporal, sense). If anger did not appear to human beings as a meaningful *experienced phenomenon* in their life world, there would be no reason to investigate it scientifically, for there would in a sense be nothing to investigate. In qualitative research in general, as in qualitative interviewing in particular, there is a primacy of the life world as experienced, since this is prior to the scientific theories we may formulate about it. This was well expressed by Maurice Merleau-Ponty, another famous phenomenologist, who built on the work of Husserl:

All my knowledge of the world, even my scientific knowledge, is gained from my own particular point of view, or from some experience of the world without which the symbols of science would be meaningless. The whole universe of science is built upon the world as directly experienced [i.e. the life world; my addition], and if we want to subject science itself to rigorous scrutiny and arrive at a precise assessment of its meaning and scope, we must begin by re-awakening the basic experiences of the world of which science is the second order expression. (Merleau-Ponty, 1945, p. ix).

Objectifying sciences give us second-order understandings of the world, but qualitative research is meant to provide a first-order understanding through concrete description.

Whether interview researchers express themselves in the idiom of phenomenology or use the language of some other qualitative paradigm (discourse analysis, symbolic interactionism, ethnomethodology, etc.), they most often decide to use interviews in order to elicit descriptions of the life world—or whatever term the given paradigm employs: the interaction order (a term used by Erving Goffman, an exponent of symbolic interactionism), or the immortal ordinary society (a term coined by Harold Garfinkel, the founder of ethnomethodology), or the set of interpretative repertoires that make something meaningful (to use the term developed by Jonathan Potter and Margaret Wetherell, significant discursive psychologists).[2]

(4) *Interpret the meaning*: Even if interviewers are generally interested in how people experience and act in the world prior to abstract theorizations, they must nonetheless often engage in interpretations of people's experiences and actions as described in interviews. One reason for this is that life world phenomena are rarely transparent and "monovocal," but are rather "polyvocal" and sometimes even contradictory, permitting multiple readings and interpretations. Who is to say what someone's description of anger signifies? Obviously, the person having experienced the anger should be listened to, but if there is one lesson to learn from 20th century human science (ranging from psychoanalysis to poststructuralism) it is that we, as human beings, do not have full authority concerning how

---

2. Obviously, these traditions are not identical, nor are their main concepts, but I believe that they here converge on the idea that there is a concretely lived and experienced social reality prior to scientific abstractions of it, which Husserl originally referred to with the notion of life world, and which remains central to most (if not all) paradigms in qualitative research.

to understand our lives, because we do not have—and can never have—full insight into the forces that have created us (Butler, 2005). We are, as Judith Butler has argued, authored by what precedes and exceeds us (p. 82), even when we are considered—as in qualitative interviews—to be authors of our own utterances. The interpretation of the meanings of the phenomena described by the interviewee can favorably be built into the conversation itself (as I tried at point [4] in the excerpt above), since this will at least give the interviewee a chance to object to a certain interpretation, but it is a process that goes on throughout an interview project (see the next chapter).

In my opinion, too rarely do interview researchers allow themselves to follow the different, polyvocal, and sometimes contradictory meanings that emerge though different voices in interviewee accounts. Analysts of interviews are generally looking for *the* voice of the interviewee, thereby ignoring internal conflicts in narratives and descriptions. Stephen Frosh has raised this concern from a discursive and psychoanalytic perspective, and he criticizes the narrativist tendency among qualitative researchers to present human experience in ways that set up coherent themes that constitute integrated wholes (Frosh, 2007). Often, it is the case that the stories that people tell are ambiguous and full of gaps, especially for people "on the margins of hegemonic discourses." (p. 637). As Butler mentioned above, Frosh finds that the human subject is never a whole, "is always riven with partial drives, social discourses that frame available modes of experience, ways of being that are contradictory and reflect the shifting allegiances of power as they play across the body and the mind." (p. 638). If this is so, it is important to be open to multiple interpretations of what is said and done in an interview. Fortunately, some qualitative approaches do have an eye to this and have designed ways to comprehend complexity, for example the so-called "listening guide," developed by Carol Gilligan and coworkers, designed to listen for multiple voices in interviewee accounts (for a recent version of this approach, see Sorsoli & Tolman, 2008).

To sum up, the "meanings" that qualitative interviewers are commonly looking for are often multiple, perspectival, and contradictory, and thus they demand careful interpretation. And there is much controversy in the qualitative communities concerning whether meanings are essentially "there," to be articulated by the interviewee and interpreted by the interviewer (emphasized in particular by phenomenological approaches), or whether meanings are constructed locally, i.e. arise dialogically in a process that centrally involves the interviewer as co-constructor (stressed by discursive and constructionist approaches). This discussion will be touched upon several times in what follows, but I shall not in this book attempt to decide once and for all how this and similar discussions should be concluded; this would indeed be overly ambitious in a short book. Rather, I shall more modestly point to a need for interviewers to make clear, when they design, conduct, and communicate their research, how they approach this thorny issue, as this will make it much easier for readers of interview reports to understand and assess what is communicated.

I have now introduced a working definition of the semi-structured qualitative research interview and emphasized four vital aspects: Such interviews are structured by the interviewer's *purpose* of obtaining knowledge; they revolve around *descriptions* provided by the interviewee; such descriptions are commonly about *life world phenomena* as experienced; and understanding the meaning of the descriptions involves some kind of *interpretation*. Although these aspects capture what is essential to a large number of qualitative interview studies now and in the past (and likely many of the future as well), we shall see that all aspects *can* be challenged, and *have* been challenged, and that there are no principles of qualitative interviewing that are always proper and correct.

In relation to qualitative interviewing, as in qualitative research in general, there is never one correct way to understand or practice a method or a technique, for everything depends on concrete circumstances and on the researcher's intentions of conducting a particular research project. This does not mean that "anything goes," and that nothing is never better than something else, but it does mean that what is "better" is always relative to what one is interested in doing or knowing. The answer to the question "What's the proper definition of and approach to qualitative interviewing?" must thus be: "It depends on what you wish to achieve by interviewing people for research purposes!" Unfortunately, too many interview researchers simply take one or another approach to interviewing for granted as the only correct one and forget to reflect sufficiently on advantages and disadvantages of their favored approach (sometimes they are not even aware that other approaches exist), and thus they proceed without properly theorizing their means of knowledge production.

Individual and Group Interviews

It is not just the interviewer's agenda and research interests that structure the interaction in an interview. Unsurprisingly, the number of interviewees also plays an important role. As the history of interviewing testifies, as recounted earlier in this chapter, the standard format of qualitative interviewing is with one person interviewing another person. This format was illustrated in the example (Box 1.1) and will be the focus of this book, but many other varieties exist that deserve to be mentioned.

- *Group interviews*: There is today an increasing use of group interviews. These have been in use since the 1920s, but became standard practice only after the 1950s, when market researchers in particular developed what they termed focus group interviews to study consumer preferences. Today, focus groups dominate consumer research and are also often used in health, education, and evaluation research, but are in fact becoming increasingly common across many disciplines in the social sciences.

In focus groups, the interviewer is conceived as a "moderator," who focuses the group discussion on specific themes of interest, and she or he will often use the group dynamic instrumentally to include a number of different perspectives on the given themes (Morgan, 2002). Often, group interviews are more dynamic and flexible in comparison with individual interviews, and they may be closer to everyday discussions. They can be used, for example, when the researcher is not so much interested in people's descriptions of their experiences as in how participants discuss, argue, and justify their opinions and attitudes.

The standard size for a focus group is between six to ten participants, led by a moderator (Chrzanowska, 2002). Recently, qualitative researchers have also experimented with groups of only two participants (sometimes referred to as "the two-person interview," although there are literally three people if the interviewer is counted), mainly because it makes the research process easier to handle than with larger groups, where people often will not show up. The moderator introduces the topics for discussion and facilitates the interchange. The point is not to reach consensus about the issues discussed, but to have different viewpoints articulated about an issue. Focus group interviews are well suited for exploratory studies in little known domains, or about newly emerging social phenomena, since the dynamic social interaction that results may provide more spontaneous expressions than in individual interviews.

• *Individual interviews*: Individual interviews with one interviewer and one interviewee may sometimes be less lively than group interviews, but they have a couple of other advantages: First, it is often easier for the interviewer in one-on-one interviews to lead the conversation in a direction that is useful in relation to the interviewer's research interests. Second, when studying aspects of people's lives that are personal, sensitive, or even taboo, it is preferable to use individual interviews that allow for more confidentiality and often make it easier for the interviewer to create an atmosphere of trust and discretion. It is very doubtful, to take a rather extreme example, that Kinsey and his colleagues could have achieved honest descriptions of sexual behaviors from their respondents, had they conducted group rather than individual interviews. And obviously there are also certain themes that just demand the presence of one person telling a story without being interrupted or gainsaid by other participants, such as in biographical research.

Although late-modern Western culture now looks upon the individual, face-to-face interview as a completely common and natural occurrence, we should be very careful not to naturalize this particular form of human relationship (i.e. to think that it is a natural and universal practice for human beings), as I emphasized above. Briggs (2007) has argued that this form of relationship implies a certain "field of communicability," referring to a socially situated construction of communicative processes (p. 556). This construction is an artifact of cultural-historical practices and is placed within organized social fields that produce different roles, positions, relations, and forms of agency that are frequently taken for granted. There are thus certain rights, duties, and a repertoire of acts that open up when entering the field of communicability of qualitative interviewing—and others that close down. Much about this field of communicability may seem trivial—that the interviewer asks questions and the interviewee answers, that the interviewee conveys personal information that he or she would not normally tell a stranger, that the interviewee is positioned as the expert on that person's own life and so on—but the role of this field in the process of knowledge production is too rarely addressed by interview researchers. We seldom stop and consider the "magic" of interviewing—that a stranger is willing to tell an interviewer so many things about her life, simply because the interviewer presents herself as a researcher. Rather than take this practice for granted, we should defamiliarize ourselves with it—like ethnographers visiting a strange "interview culture"—in order to understand and appreciate its role in scientific knowledge production.

Interviewing Using Different Media

Following from Briggs' analysis of the communicability of interviewing, it is noteworthy that the otherwise standardized format of "face-to-face interaction" was only named early in the 20th century by the sociologist Charles Horton Cooley (see Briggs, 2007, p. 553), but was since considered as "primordial, authentic, quintessentially human, and necessary." (p. 553). It is sometimes forgotten that the face-to-face interview is also a kind of interaction that is mediated by this particular social arrangement that has a history. Other well-known media employed in qualitative interviewing include the telephone and the Internet, and we shall now take a brief look at differences between face-to-face, telephone, and Internet interviews.

• *Face-to-face interviews*: In face-to-face interviews people are present not only as conversing minds, but as flesh and blood creatures that may laugh, cry, smile, tremble, and otherwise give away much information in terms of gestures, body language, and facial expressions. Interviewers thus have the richest source of knowledge available here, but the challenge concerns how to use it productively. In most cases, how people look and act is forgotten once the transcript is made, and the researcher carries out her analyses using the stack of transcripts rather than the embodied interaction that took place. This is a problem especially when a research assistant, or someone else who was not the interviewer, transcribes the interview, because in that case, it is not possible to note and recall all the nonverbal signs and gestures that occurred. If possible, it is therefore preferable for the interviewer herself to transcribe the conversations, and it is optimal to do so relatively soon after the conversations are over (e.g. within a couple of days), since this guarantees better recollection of the body language, the atmosphere, and other such nontranscribable features of the interaction.

• *Telephone interviews*: According to Shuy (2002), the telephone interview has "swept the polling and survey industry in recent years and is now the dominant approach" (p. 539)—often in a very structured format (as was discussed above). In a research context, the use of telephone conversations was pioneered by conversation analysts, who were able to identify a number of common conversational mechanisms (related to turn-taking, adjacency pairs such as questions-answers, etc.) from the rather constricted format that is possible over the telephone. The constricted format itself may have been productive in throwing light on certain core features of human talk.

Shuy emphasizes a number of advantages of telephone interviewing, such as reduced interviewer effects (important in structured polling interviews, for example), better interviewer uniformity, greater standardization of questions, greater cost-efficiency, increased researcher safety (Shuy, 2002, p. 540), and—we might add—better opportunities for interviewing people who live far away from the interviewer. In qualitative interviewing, it is not possible (nor desirable) to avoid "interviewer effects," because the interviewer herself is the research instrument, so only the latter couple of points are relevant in this context. However, Shuy also highlights some advantages of in-person interviewing as against telephone interviewing, such as more accurate responses due to contextual naturalness, greater likelihood of self-generated answers, more symmetrical distribution of interactive power, greater effectiveness with complex issues, more thoughtful responses, and the fact that face-to-face interviews are better in relation to sensitive questions (pp. 541–544). The large majority of interviews that are characterized as "qualitative" are conducted face-to-face, mainly because of these advantages listed by Shuy.

• *Internet interviews*: E-mail and chat interviews are varieties of Internet interviewing with e-mail interviewing normally implying an asynchronous interaction in time, with the interviewer writing a question and then waiting for a response, and chat interviews being synchronous or "real time" (Mann & Stewart, 2002). The latter can approach a conversational format that resembles face-to-face interviews with quick turn-takings. When doing online ethnographies, e.g. in virtual realities on the Internet, chat interviews are important (see Markham, 2005, on online ethnography). One advantage of e-mail and chat interviews is that they are "self-transcribing" in the sense that the written text itself is the medium through which researcher and respondents express themselves, and the text is thus basically ready for analysis the minute it has been typed (Kvale & Brinkmann, 2008, p. 149).

Disadvantages of such interview forms are related to the demanded skills of written communication. Many people are not sufficiently skilled at writing to be able to express themselves in rich and detailed ways. Most research participants are more comfortable when talking, rather than writing, about their lives and experiences. However, as the psychiatrist Finn Skårderud has pointed out, there are some exceptions here, and Skårderud emphasizes in particular that Internet conversations can be useful when communicating with people who have problematic relationships to their bodies (e.g. eating disorders). For such people, the physical presence of a problematic body can represent an unwanted disturbance (Skårderud, 2003).

In discussing the different media of interviewing, it should be emphasized that all interviews are mediated, even if only by the spoken words and the historical arrangement of questioning through face-to-face interaction, and there is no universally correct medium that will always guarantee success. Interviewers should choose their medium according to their knowledge interests, and should at a minimum reflect on the effects of communicating through one medium rather than another. That said, most of the themes that qualitative interviewers are interested in lend themselves more easily to face-to-face interviewing because of the trust, confidentiality, and contextual richness that this format enables.

Different Styles of Interviewing

We have now seen how interviews may differ in terms of structure, number of participants, and media. Another crucial factor is the style of interviewing, i.e. the way the interviewer acts and positions herself in the conversation. In relation to this, Wengraf (2001) has introduced a helpful distinction between receptive and assertive interviewer styles (or strategies, as he calls them), with the former being close to Carl Rogers's model of psychotherapy, and the latter being more in line with active and perhaps Socratic approaches to interviewing, both of which were briefly addressed in the historical section above.

• *Receptive interviewing*: According to Wengraf, a receptive style empowers informants and enables them to have "a large measure of control in the way in which they answer the relatively few and relatively open questions they are asked." (Wengraf, 2001, p. 155). Much of what was said above on the historical contributions by Elton Mayo and Carl Rogers, and also the sections on semi-structured life-world interviewing, broadly addressed the receptive style—which is often thought of as self-evidently right, so that no alternatives are considered. Therefore, I shall devote more space to articulate the somewhat more unusual assertive style.

• *Assertive interviewing*: Wengraf states that an assertive style may come close to a legal interrogation and enables the interviewer "to control the responses, provoke and illuminate self-contradiction, absences, provoke self-reflexivity and development" (2001, p. 155), perhaps approaching transformative conceptions of interviewing in Roulston's terminology.

A well-known exposition of the assertive style was developed by Holstein and Gubrium in their book on *The Active Interview* (Holstein & Gubrium, 1995). They argued that there is in reality not much of a choice, because interviews are unavoidably—in their eyes—interpretively active, meaning-making practices, and this would apply even for interviewers attempting a more receptive style. (Perhaps their role in meaning-making would just be more elusive and more difficult to take into account when analyzing interview talk.) A consequence of this line of argument could be that it would be preferable for interviewers to take into account their inevitable role as co-constructors of meaning rather than trying to downplay it.

Discourse analysts such as Potter and Wetherell (1987) have also developed an active, assertive practice of interviewing. In a classic text, they describe the constructive role of the interview researcher and summarize discourse analytic interviewing as follows:

First, variation in response is as important as consistency. Second, techniques which allow diversity rather than those which eliminate it are emphasized, resulting in more informal conversational exchanges and third, interviewers are seen as active participants rather than like speaking questionnaires. (Potter & Wetherell, 1987, p. 165).

Variation, diversity, informality, and an active interviewer are the key words, and the interview process, for Potter and Wetherell, is meant to lead to articulations of the "interpretative repertoires" of the interviewees, but without the interviewer investigating the legitimacy of these repertoires in the interview situation or the respondent's ways of justifying them. This is in contrast to Socratic and other confronting variants of active interviews, which are designed not just to map participants' understandings and beliefs, but also to study the extent to which participants can justify their understandings and beliefs.

In order to illustrate concretely what an assertive style of the confronting kind looks like, we may turn to a simple and very short example from Plato's *The Republic* with Socrates as interviewer (discussed in Brinkmann, 2007a). The passage very elegantly demonstrates that no moral rules are self-applying or self-interpreting, but must always be understood contextually. Socrates is in a conversation with Cephalus, who believes that justice (*dikaiosune*)—here "doing right"—can be stated in universal rules, such as "tell the truth" and "return borrowed items":

'That's fair enough, Cephalus,' I [Socrates] said. 'But are we really to say that doing right consists simply and solely in truthfulness and returning anything we have borrowed? Are those not actions that can be sometimes right and sometimes wrong? For instance, if one borrowed a weapon from a friend who subsequently went out of his mind and then asked for it back, surely it would be generally agreed that one ought not to return it, and that it would not be right to do so, not to consent to tell the strict truth to a madman?'
'That is true,' he [Cephalus] replied.
'Well then, I [Socrates] said, 'telling the truth and returning what we have borrowed is not the definition of doing right.' (Plato, 1987, pp. 65–66).

Here, the conversation is interrupted by Polemarchus who disagrees with Socrates' preliminary conclusion, and Cephalus quickly leaves in order to go to a sacrifice. Then Polemarchus takes Cephalus' position as Socrates' discussion partner and the conversation continues as if no substitution had happened.

The passage is instructive, because it shows us what qualitative interviewing normally is *not*. For Socrates violates almost every standard principle of qualitative research interviewing, and we can see that the conversation is a great contrast to my own interview above (Box 1.1). First, we can see that Socrates talks much more than his respondent. There is some variety across the dialogues concerning how much Socrates talks in comparison with the other participants, but the example given here, where Socrates develops an absurd conclusion from the initial belief voiced by Cephalus, is not unusual, although the balance is much more equal in other places. Second, Socrates has not asked Cephalus to "describe a situation in which he has experienced justice" or "tell a story about doing right from his own experience" or a similar concretely descriptive question, probing for "lived experience." Instead, they are talking about the definition of an important general concept. Third, Socrates contradicts and challenges his respondent's view. He is not a warm and caring conversationalist. Fourth, there is no debriefing or attempt to make sure that the interaction was a pleasant experience for Cephalus. Fifth, the interview is conducted in public rather than private, and the topic is not private experiences or biographical details, but justice, a theme of common human interest, at least of interest to all citizens of Athens. Sixth, and perhaps most importantly, the interview here is radically anti-psychologistic. It does not make much difference whether the conversation partner is Cephalus or Polemarchus—and the discussion continues in exactly the same way after Cephalus has left. The crux of the discussion is whether the participants are able to give good reasons for their belief in a public discussion, not whether they have this or that biographical background or have had a certain experience or not.

The formal structure of this kind of active interview has been mapped by Dinkins:

1. Socrates encounters someone who takes an action or makes a statement into which Socrates wishes to inquire.
2. Socrates asks the person for a definition of the relevant central concept, which is then offered.
3. Together, Socrates and the respondent (or "co-inquirer" to use Dinkins' term) deduce some consequences of the definition.

4. Socrates points out a possible conflict between the deduced consequences and another belief held by the respondent. The respondent is then given the choice of rejecting the belief or the definition.
5. Usually, the respondent rejects the definition, because the belief is too central—epistemically or existentially—to be given up.
6. A new definition is offered, and the steps are repeated (adapted from Dinkins, 2005, p. 124).

Sometimes, the conversation partners in the Platonic dialogues settle on a definition, but more often the dialogue ends without any final, unarguable definition of the central concept (e.g. justice, virtue, love). This lack of resolution—*aporia* in Greek—can be interpreted as illustrating the open-ended character of our conversational reality, including the open-ended character of the discursively produced knowledge of human social and historical life. If humankind is a kind of enacted conversation, to return to my opening remarks in this chapter, the goal of social science is perhaps not to arrive at "fixed knowledge" once and for all, but to help human beings improve the quality of their conversational reality, to help them know their own society and social practices and debate the goals and values that are important in their lives (Flyvbjerg, 2001).

Interviews can be intentionally assertive, active and confronting (good examples are found in Bellah, Madsen, Sullivan, Swidler & Tipton, 1985, who explicitly acknowledge a debt to Socrates), but the assertive approach can also be employed *post hoc* as a more analytic perspective. Consider, for example, the following excerpt in Box 1.2 from a study by Shweder and Much (1987), discussed in detail by Valsiner (2007, pp. 385–386). The interview is set in India and was part of a research project studying moral reasoning cross-culturally. Earlier in the interview, Babaji (the interviewee) was presented with a variant of the famous Heinz dilemma (here called the Ashok dilemma), invented by moral developmental psychologist Lawrence Kohlberg to assess people's moral capabilities (Kohlberg, 1981): A man (Heinz/Ashok) has a wife who is ill and will die if he does not steal some medicine from a pharmacist (who refuses to sell the medicine at a price that the man can afford). According to Babaji's Hinduism, stealing is not permitted, and the interview unfolds from there:

Box 1.2 **An Interview on Hindu Morality**

Interviewer: Why doesn't Hindu dharma permit stealing?

Babaji: If he steals, it is a sin—so what virtue is there in saving a life. Hindu dharma keeps man from sinning.

Interviewer: Why would it be a sin? Isn't there a saying "One must jump into fire for others"?

Babaji: That is there in our dharma—sacrifice, but not stealing.

Interviewer: But if he doesn't provide the medicine for his wife, she will die. Wouldn't it be a sin to let her die?

Babaji: That's why, according to the capacities and powers which God has given him, he should try to give her shamanistic instructions and advice. Then she can be cured.

Interviewer: But, that particular medicine is the only way out.

Babaji: There is no reason to necessarily think that that particular drug will save her life.

Interviewer: Let's suppose she can only be saved by that drug, or else she will die. Won't he face lots of difficulties if his wife dies?

Babaji: No.

Interviewer: But his family will break up.

Babaji: He can marry other women.

Interviewer: But he has no money. How can he remarry?

Babaji: Do you think he should steal? If he steals, he will be sent to jail. Then what's the use of saving her life to keep the family together. She has enjoyed the days destined for her. But stealing is bad. Our sacred scriptures tell that sometimes stealing is an act of dharma. If by stealing for you I can save your life, then it is an act of dharma. But one cannot steal for his wife or his offspring or for himself. If he does that, it is simply stealing.

Interviewer: If I steal for myself, then it's a sin?

Babaji: Yes.

Interviewer: But in this case I am stealing for my wife, not for me.

Babaji: But your wife is yours.

Interviewer: Doesn't Ashok have a duty or obligation to steal the drug?

Babaji: He may not get the medicine by stealing. He may sell himself. He may sell himself to someone for say 500 rupees for six months or one year. (Shweder & Much, 1987, p. 236).

According to Valsiner (2007), we see in the interview how the interviewer (Richard Shweder), in a very active or assertive way, does everything he can to persuade Babaji to accept the Western framing of the dilemma and see the tension between stealing for a moral reason and stealing as an immoral act. But Babaji fails to (or actively refuses to) see the situation as a dilemma and first attempts to articulate other possibilities in addition to stealing/not stealing (viz. give shamanistic instructions) before finally suggesting that Ashok sell himself in order to raise the money. As such, the interview flow is best understood as an active and confrontational encounter between two quite different worldviews that are revealed exactly because the interviewer acts in a confronting, although not disrespectful, way.[3]

Furthermore, the excerpt illustrates how cross-cultural interviewing can be quite difficult—but also extremely interesting—not least when conducted in "noninterview societies" (Ryen, 2002, p. 337), i.e., in societies where interviewing is not common or recognized as a knowledge-producing instrument. All qualitative interviewing is a collaborative accomplishment, but this becomes exceedingly visible when collaborating cross-culturally.

Analytic Approaches to Interviewing

Before closing this chapter, I shall give a brief introduction to different analytic approaches to interviewing, once again ordered by a simplified dichotomy, which should really be thought of as a continuum. I will introduce explicitly a distinction that has played an implicit role above between interview talk as primarily descriptive phenomenological *reports* (concentrating on the "what" of communication) and interview talk as primarily discursive *accounts* (chiefly concerned with the "how" of talk). Phenomenological approaches to interviewing (exemplified in my exposition above of semi-structured life-world

---

3. Confronting interviews are sometimes misunderstood to imply a certain aggressive or disrespectful attitude, which, of course, is a misunderstanding. An interviewer can be actively and confrontingly curious and inquiring in a very respectful way, especially if she positions herself as not-knowing (ad modum Socrates in some of the dialogues) in order to avoid framing the interview as an oral examination.

interviewing) try to get as close as possible to precise descriptions of *what* people have experienced; other analytical approaches (found, for example, in certain schools of discourse analysis and conversation analysis) focus on *how* people express themselves and give accounts occasioned by the situation in which they find themselves. The two approaches are contrasted in Table 1.1 below.

Inspiration for slicing the cake of qualitative interviewing in this manner comes from Talmy (2010) and Rapley (2001), who builds on a distinction from Seale between interview-data-as-resource and interview-data-as-topic.

• *Interviews as research instruments:* Researchers working from the former perspective (interview-data-as-resource—corresponding to the left hand side of the Table) believe that interview data can reflect the interviewees' reality outside the interview. They consequently seek to minimize the interviewer's effects on coloring interviewees' reports of their reality. The interview becomes a research instrument in the hands of interviewers, who are supposed to act receptively in order to interfere as little as possible with the interviewee reporting. The validity of the interviewees' reports becomes a prime issue when one approaches interviewing primarily as a research instrument. And since interviews

Table 1.1

Interviewing as a research instrument and as social practice

Conception of interviewing	Research instrument	Social practice
Conception of interview data	Reports, interview data as resource	Accounts, interview data as topics
Standard analytic focus	Lived experience— the "what"	Situated interaction— the "how"
Typical interviewer style	Receptive	Assertive
Main challenge	Validity of interviewee reports	Relevance of interviewee accounts
Paradigmatic background	Phenomenology, Grounded Theory etc.	Discourse analysis, Conversation Analysis etc.

normally concern things experienced in the past, this significantly involves considerations about human memory, and about how to enhance the trustworthiness of human recollections.

In one of the few publications to discuss the role of memory in interviewing, Thomsen and Brinkmann (2009) recommend that interviewers take the following points into account if they want to help interviewees' improve the reporting of specific memories:

- Allow time for recall and assure the interviewee that this is normal.
- Provide concrete cues, e.g. "the last time you were talking to a physician/nurse" rather than "a communication experience."
- Use typical content categories of specific memories to derive cues (i.e. ongoing activity, location, persons, other people's affect and own affect).
- Ask for recent specific memories.
- Use relevant extended time line and landmark events as contextual cues, i.e. "when you were working at x" to aid the recall of older memories.
- Ask the interviewee for a free and detailed narrative of the specific memory. (adapted from Thomsen & Brinkmann, 2009).

Following such guidelines is meant to result in interviewee descriptions that are valid (which means that they are about what the researcher intends them to be about), and close to the "lived experience" of something, or what was called experiences of life world phenomena earlier in the chapter. Although phenomenology is one typical paradigm to frame interviews analytically as research instruments, many other paradigms do so as well, for example Grounded Theory, which has been developed since Glaser and Strauss (1967) with the intent of developing theoretical understandings of phenomena grounded in empirical materials with meticulous coding of data being a significant technique.

- *Interviewing as a social practice*: In contrast to approaches that see interviewing as a research instrument designed to capture the "what" of what is reported as accurately as possible, researchers working from more constructionist, localist, and situated perspectives have much greater analytic focus on the "how" of interviewing. They view interviewing as a social practice; as a site for a specific kind of situated interaction, which means that interview data primarily reflect "a reality constructed by the interviewee and interviewer." (Rapley, 2001, p. 304). The idea of obtaining valid reports that accurately reflect a reality outside the conversational situation is thus questioned, and the main challenge becomes instead how to explain the relevance of interview talk. That is, if what is said in an interview is a product of this social practice itself, how can it ever be relevant to conduct interviewing? Postmodern interviews, emphasizing performative and transformative aspects of interviewing, represent attempts to meet this challenge by arguing that if interviews do not concern a reality outside themselves, they can instead be used to perform or facilitate social change.

People subscribing to the right hand side of Table 1 believe that interview talk should be conceived as accounts. Unlike reports, which refer to experiences in the interviewee's past that can be articulated when prompted, accounts are answers that are "normatively oriented to and designed for the questions that occasion them" (Talmy, 2010, p. 136). If interviewee talk is best understood as accounts, it must be seen as a kind of social action that has effects and *does* something in the situation of which it is a part. This perspective on interviewing is shared by some discourse analysts and conversation analysts, who limit themselves to analyzing interview talk as situated interaction; I return to this in later chapters and provide an example.

Readers may wonder at this point how two approaches that are so different can coexist in the same book. My own pragmatic answer is that none of the approaches should be brought to an extreme: It is true that there are huge problems associated with viewing the interview as a site for pure reports of the past (we know too much about the constructive role of human memory, and of how the social practice of interviewing mediates what is said, to take this seriously). But it is certainly also true that there are problems associated with denying that we can refer more or less accurately to past experiences (and those who follow the right-hand side of Table 1, and deny that interview data can be a resource for understanding experiences of the past, nevertheless believe that their own communicative practice, materialized in their texts, are about matters outside this specific text, i.e., they believe—quite reasonably—that they can use words to refer to a reality beyond their words).

So, taken to extremes, both approaches become absurd, and I believe that it is now time for the two (sometimes opposed) camps to learn from one another and realize that they need not exclude one another. In my view, some of the most interesting interview studies are those where analyses of the "what" and the "how" fertilize each other in productive ways. I will end this chapter with a brief illustration of this taken (rather shamelessly!) from a paper coauthored by myself (Musaeus & Brinkmann, 2011) that shows how an analytic look at interviews can employ perspectives from both sides at the same time. The two forms thus need not exclude each other, and some interviews can favorably be analyzed using a combination of the two broad analytic approaches.

First a little bit of contextualization to render the excerpt meaningful: My colleague, Peter Musaeus (the first author of the article that reports the study), conducted a group qualitative interview with four members of a family (in their home) that was receiving family therapy. We were interested in understanding the effects of the therapeutic process on the everyday life of the family. In the excerpt in Box 1.3 below, we meet Maren and Søren, a married couple, and Maren's daughter Kirstina, who was 13 years old at the time, in addition to the interviewer.[4] In the following extract, Maren (the mother) has just made a joke about the movie *The Planet of the Apes* (a science-fiction movie telling the story of how apes are in control of the Earth and keep humans as pets or slaves), and they have talked about the scene where the apes jokingly remark that females are cute, just as long as you get rid of them before puberty.

---

4. Kirstina has an older sister, who no longer lives at home, and Søren is not the biological father of the girls. He has two children from a previous marriage, one of whom has attempted suicide, which, however, is not the reason for the family's referral to therapy. The reason, instead, is Maren's violent behavior towards her daughter Kirstina.

Box 1.3 **A Family Interview**

1 Maren: And the comment that followed was: "Get rid of it before...ha, ha="
2 Interviewer: Before it becomes a teenager?
3 Maren: Because it simply is so hard.
4 Interviewer: Yes, right, but it=
5 Kirstina: Should you also simply get rid of me?
6 Interviewer: Ha, ha.
7 Maren: No, are you crazy, I love you more than anything. But it's really hard
8 for all of us sometimes, I think.
9 Kirstina: Are you also in puberty when you hit me?
10 Maren: No, I am in the menopause, that is different.
11 Interviewer: Ha, ha.
12 Søren: You don't hit, do you? You say "when you hit"? Your mother doesn't
13 hit you.
14 Kirstina: She has hit me today and yesterday.
15 Maren: I probably did hit her but well=
16 Kirstina: Yes, but still, you may say that it isn't hitting, when you miss.
17 Søren: STOP Kirstina, it isn't true. Your mother hasn't hit you and you don't
18 hit.
19 Kirstina: No, no let's just say that.
20 Maren: Does anyone want a cream roll? (adapted from Musaeus & Brinkmann, 2011, p. 53).

Toward the end of this sequence, Søren, the father of the family, denies—as he does throughout the interview—that Maren is hitting her daughter, and he uses what the family calls a "stop sign" (line 17), which they were taught to employ in their therapy sessions. The verbal sign "STOP" (said in a loud voice) is supposed to bring the conflict cycle to a halt before it accelerates. In the interview, however, the stop sign (like other similar signs from therapy that have been appropriated by the family members) sometimes functions counterproductively to raise the conflict level, as it is almost shouted by the family members. The sudden question in line 20 is actually much more effective in halting the conflict, diverting the participants' attention from the problem.

I have here provided just a glimpse of our analysis, which tries to bring forth the role of semiotic mediation, i.e. the use of signs (like the stop sign and other therapeutic tools) in regulating social interaction in a troubled family. The interview contains family members' descriptions of their problems and challenges, thus giving us *reports* of what they experience, but we also see the family members' shared past being formative of the present in the interview situation itself, resulting in quite significant *accounts* occasioned by the social episode itself. In short, the two analytic perspectives on interviewing (both as a resource providing reports and also as a topic in its own right, i.e. a social practice in which accounts are given) are mutually reinforcing in this case, and have given us what we (the authors of the paper) believe is a valid analysis. Rather than just hearing people describing their problems, the interviewer was witnessing the family members' problems as they played out in their interaction, offering him a chance to validate his analysis.

Conclusions

In this chapter, I have given a broad introduction to qualitative interviewing. I have tried to demonstrate that the human world is a conversational reality in which interviewing takes a privileged position as a research method, at least in relation to a number of significant research questions that human and social scientists want to ask. Qualitative interviewing can be both a useful and a valid approach, resulting in analyses with a certain objectivity in the sense that I introduced above. Throughout the chapter, I have kept an eye on interviewing as a social practice that has a cultural history, and I have warned against unreflective "naturalization" of this kind of human interaction, i.e., viewing it as a particularly natural and unproblematic way of staging human relationships.

Furthermore, I introduced a number of distinctions that are relevant when mapping the field of qualitative interviewing, e.g. between different levels of structure, different numbers of participants, different media of interviewing, and also different interviewer styles. Other distinctions will be introduced in the rest of the book whenever they are relevant. I also provided a detailed presentation of semi-structured life-world interviewing, as the standard form of qualitative interviewing today.

I finally gave particular attention to two broad analytic approaches to interviewing: On the one side, experience-focused interviewing seeking to elicit accurate reports of what interviewees have experienced (in broad terms the phenomenological positions), and on the other side, language- and interaction-focused interviewing (discourse-oriented positions) that focus on the nature of interview interaction in its own right.

In my eyes, none of these approaches is superior *per se*, but they enable researchers to pose different kinds of questions to their materials. Too often, however, interviewers forget to make clear what kinds of questions they are interested in, and also forget to consider whether their practice of interviewing and their analytic focus enable them to answer their research questions satisfactorily. This will be a recurring theme in the following chapters on research design, on writing up the methods section, and also on writing up the research findings.

2

RESEARCH DESIGN IN INTERVIEW STUDIES

AS IN any other genre of science, research using qualitative interviewing does not just happen by chance, but is designed by researchers. What sets research interviews apart from everyday conversations is the much greater extent to which they are planned and reflected upon in advance—and subsequently analyzed. In everyday life, we generally just follow the conversational flows with the people we meet, but qualitative interviews are prepared, conducted, analyzed, and reported according to some kind of plan or what is normally referred to as a research design. Some designs imply a tight structuring of the research process while others are much more loose and flexible, but even the most stretchy and negotiable design is still a design (which serves some purposes better than others). In other words, my claim is that one cannot *not* design an interview study, for even the conscious choice of omitting any preparation and just talking to people around one about something is also to have chosen a design (which, in most cases, however, will probably not be conducive to knowledge production).

In this chapter, I will discuss a number of issues that should be taken into account when considering research designs in qualitative interviewing. I outline a well tried-out step-wise approach to design that is informative of *what* to do, *when* to do it, and *why* do this rather than that in the research process. I will introduce some conceptual distinctions between inductive, deductive, and abductive designs, and I shall refer to three examples from paradigmatic interview studies to show more concretely how different designs enable different research processes and results. Some projects are designed for discovery and generally demand a quite disciplined analytic awareness, while others are designed more for understanding something and come close to ethnographic research that seeks to take advantage of whatever conversations emerge in the field that the researcher is interested in. It is also possible to design a study in order to construct something new (new practices or new kinds of public discussions).

Going Through an Interview Study

Some approaches to interviewing focus almost exclusively on the concrete encounter between an interviewer and an interviewee. In contrast to this, I will here argue that a well-designed interview project has a thread that runs through the entire process and connects the research question with what goes on in the interview and also with subsequent transcription, analysis, and reporting. Thus, when designing an interview study, and also when readers evaluate the appropriateness of different designs, it can be helpful to think through the process in a step-wise manner. Here I break the process down into four common steps: *Preparation, interviewing, analysis*, and *reporting*.

These should not be thought of as discrete phases, but are generally overlapping and cyclic, so that one may, for example, return to one's interviewees and conduct additional interviews after having analyzed their initial statements, or even re-thematize the entire project upon recognizing that the project has come off to a misguided start and in fact concerns something other than one had first imagined. Whether one prefers tight or loose designs, one should always make the best of the flexible and inductive research logic that normally guides qualitative research. This makes possible an iterative design—a form of designing-as-we-go-along—which is normally a vice in quantitative and experimental research, where the 99th research participant must be treated in exactly the same way as the 1st participant in order to ensure reliability. But in qualitative research, it can be a virtue to amend one's design in the process. It would be foolish to continue with a bad interview guide that does not result in valid answers, for example, if it turns out after a couple of interviews that the guide is problematic. Of course, any amendments should be carefully noted and reflected upon (and when relevant, should also be mentioned in the final report), and it is advisable for interview researchers to use a log book to keep track of the decisions that are made throughout the process, as these are often difficult to reconstruct correctly in hindsight.

Preparation

The first thing to consider when preparing an interview study is to make clear what one wants to study. What is the theme that one is interested in? People's life stories, experiences, or actions? The second thing is to consider whether qualitative interviewing is suitable for the given research theme. In their book on designing qualitative research, Marshall and Rossman (2006) argue that there are three broad areas of study to which qualitative methods can favorably be applied (p. 55):

- Individual lived experience.
- Language and communication.
- Society and culture.

Qualitative interviews can be used, and have been used, to study aspects of all three, but they lend themselves most naturally to the study of individual lived experience. In fact, when one wants to know how an individual experiences some phenomenon, interviewing has a certain primacy among the different methods. Interviews can also be used to study language and communication, since human beings use the interview situation itself to communicate through language. But generalizing from communicative processes in the interview situation to the broader world of human communication is a thorny issue. If one wants to study "naturally occurring talk" (e.g. how doctors communicate with patients), it can be important to obtain naturalistic data rather than just interviewing people about how they believe they communicate outside the interview context. Finally, since society and culture are co-constituted by conversational processes such as interviews, qualitative interviewing remains a relevant method for studying these aspects of the social world; but, again, it can be quite important to use other sources of data (e.g. observations, documents, cultural objects) to get a more complete picture. Qualitative interviewing is very often a relevant method, but it is not always a sufficient method vis-à-vis the phenomenon of interest.

It is not uncommon, however, to find that people have fallen in love with interviewing as a method, and then seek to apply it to answer questions that are ill-suited for this kind of method. Judging from my experience as a teacher of qualitative interviewing, it happens quite often that novice interviewers want to know, for example, if it makes a difference (in relation to a given subject matter) whether people are men or women, young or old, or homosexual or heterosexual. In small projects, they then recruit, say, two women and two men and ask them about their opinions about something. There is nothing intrinsically wrong with this, but the problem arises when the researchers want to use this limited material to draw conclusions about general differences between men and women (for example). For, obviously, it is entirely possible that the selected men have opinions that are stereotypically associated with women (and vice versa).

The problem is that interviewers very often have inherited a research logic taken from experimental research and see this as *the* scientific method, intent, as it is, to investigate differences between groups. So they wish to have a "control group," let us say of men, in order to verify whether their understandings of women are valid. This runs counter to a genuine qualitative research logic, and in fact makes very little sense. If I want to make an interpretation of the works of William Shakespeare, it would be quite strange to demand that I use Homer or Dante as controls. Or, if I were to conduct fieldwork in rural Russia, what sense would there be in demanding that I use an urban area in the United States as a control? Naturally, it can be very interesting to do comparative studies in qualitative research (as the study described in Box 2.2 below will exemplify), but this must be done in very careful, analytic ways and is usually quite different from testing a hypothesis about general differences between groups. Qualitative interviewers need to be aware that qualitative research functions differently from experimental research, and that the whole idea of using controls in this way normally makes little sense.

In qualitative interviewing, we should in general pose research questions that contain a "how" instead of a "how much." A research question such as "How do young people experience being admitted to hospital?" is generally preferable to the comparative question "Are women more anxious than men when admitted to hospital?" The latter question invites us to think in terms of causes, effects, and control groups, and in order to answer the question in a statistical sense, one would need a large number of interviewees. A question like "How do people cope with the loss of a loved one?" is in general better for qualitative projects than questions that seek to find causal effects, such as "Does psychotherapy reduce the risk of depression after a loss?" The latter question is interesting and relevant, but it is also extremely difficult to answer with qualitative interviewing. Instead, one would need to enlist a large number of research participants, administrate standardized tests, and compare the effects statistically in order to assess whether the findings are statistically significant, i.e., not just a chance result. In most cases, it is relevant to conduct qualitative interviews when one wants to know about how people experience something, reason about something, or act in relation to something. The result of an interview study may well be (and often is) that people do so in different ways (and the researcher can for example construct a typology of ways of experiencing, reasoning, or acting in order to show this), but this is different from saying that being a man/woman is causing one to experience something in a given way.

Design questions that should be answered when preparing an interview study are generally of five broad kinds: *What* should be studied? *Why* is it relevant to do so? *How* should the subject matter be studied? *Who* should be interviewed—and *how many*? I will deal with each question in turn.

• *What* should be studied? The question of *what* should always be addressed before the question of which methods to use. One should employ the methods that suit the theme rather than skew the theme to make it fit preconceived ideas about methods. As discussed above, the strength of qualitative interviewing is its ability to throw light on the *hows* of human action and experience: How is something *done* (e.g. patienthood), and how is something *experienced* (e.g. anxiety) can favorably be studied using qualitative interviewing. So, in general, it is helpful to formulate one's research interest in terms of a list of hows. At this stage, it is also relevant to reflect upon methodology in a more overarching way—for example, is the researcher aiming to discover something unknown about how people do X, to construct a better way of doing X, or to understand how people experience X? (I return to the models of *discovery, construction,* and *understanding* below). It is also relevant to consider the philosophy of science that one adheres to (implicitly or explicitly). There can be quite a difference between approaching the human world as a range of conversational exchanges (a perspective found in discourse analysis and conversation analysis, for example), and conceiving of the human world as a reality that is structured by intentional acts of human consciousness (a perspective found in parts of phenomenology, for example).

• *Why* is it relevant to study this? The human world is rich and varied, and it is possible to raise an endless number of questions that can be answered using qualitative interviewing. But not all questions are equally relevant, and I believe that there is an ethical obligation to use the privileges one has as a researcher to study phenomena that are relevant, and where there might even be a chance that the results of the study may improve the world (however little this may be). This is not to say that all research projects should be directly relevant to a certain practice, for example, for basic research also may be very enlightening for human beings. Sometimes it is the case that what initially appears "useless" may turn out to be the most useful. But most readers of interview reports will quite legitimately expect the qualitative researcher to have given thought to why this piece of research is relevant, and to whom it might be relevant. As the critical psychologist Ian Parker has put it, as researchers we are "always participating in the activity of either reproducing the way the world is or transforming it" (Parker, 2005, p. 13), and there can be quite a difference between designing for reproduction and designing for transformation. Should the interviewees, for example, be expected to be enlightened and lead better lives upon having participated in the study? And what are the ethical challenges in this kind of transformative research (cf. the discussion of transformative interviewing in Chapter 1)?

Furthermore, qualitative inquiry has grown and expanded and is now an enormous field, and it is very often the case that other researchers have already studied the phenomenon that one is interested in. Has the researcher done an adequate literature review that enables her to assess whether her own questions may contribute with something new? "Because I can!" is not a good answer when asked about why you want to study something, and there is in today's qualitative research—as in all other forms of research as well—an enormous amount of repetitions that do not teach us anything substantially new. The sad truth is that one specific implicit answer to why it is relevant to study something is dominant, viz. that it is relevant because the researcher has an aim of getting tenure or living up to a publication pressure. In such cases, it can be argued that the researcher could make better use of her time by studying something that could actually make a difference to people (and hopefully enable her to get tenure in the process!).

Someone who has put a lot of emphasis on the relevance aspects of human and social science is Bent Flyvbjerg (2001). In a book on how to make the social sciences matter (i.e. how to make them *relevant*), he has argued that the social sciences must become *phronetic*, which means that they must conceive of themselves as practical sciences that are involved in the societal subject matters that they study. *Phronetic* researchers place themselves within the context being studied and focus on the values of the practices of communities by asking three "value-rational" questions: Where are we going? Is this desirable? What should be done? (p. 60). The raison d'être for the social sciences, Flyvbjerg thinks, is developing the value-rationality of society, i.e., enabling the public to reason better about its values and social practices. This is just one approach to the why-question of qualitative studies, which argues that, ideally, qualitative research is valid when it enables people to improve the practice that is studied.

As a bridge between "why" and "how," it is also relevant to consider the ethical aspects of interview research. Ethical aspects concern both the *why*, as we have seen, and obviously also the *how*, since research should proceed concretely in an ethically sound manner. This involves asking questions about one's own project. These questions include:

Possible *beneficial* consequences of the study: Can the study improve the lives of human beings in any way?

How to obtain *informed consent*. This can be a challenge in qualitative interviewing, since researchers often develop and change their focus in the course of the research process, sometimes making it necessary to inform participants about changes in the direction of the research process and to ask them for renewed consent.

How to protect participants' *confidentiality*. This is particularly relevant in qualitative inquiry, where researchers often deal with intimate aspects of people's lives.

The *consequences* of the study for the participants: Is there a risk that they can be harmed psychologically by taking part in the study, e.g. by engaging in conversations about painful experiences from the past?

In many countries, it is demanded that researchers obtain approval from an ethics committee (often institutionalized at local universities), but it is important not to reduce ethical issues to a "check-list approach," so that one simply goes ahead without further reflection after having gained formal approval. In qualitative research, unexpected ethical questions can easily arise, and it is important to remain open to these questions throughout a project rather than believing that ethical questions can be dealt with once and for all before a project is initiated. In any case, most readers of interview reports would like to know something about how the researcher has handled the four ethical issues mentioned here.

- *How* should the subject matter be studied? The question of how is clearly the biggest one, where both theoretical and methodological questions must be raised. Should the interviews be conducted to capture "lived experience" or should they be seen as a form of situated interaction in their own right, for example? Also, more concrete and practical questions must be raised, such as: How can the research questions be translated into an interview guide that makes sense to the interviewees?

The *how* questions cannot of course be answered abstractly, but only concretely, depending on what one wants to find out by conducting the study. The particular context and practicalities of the study are here of paramount importance. If the researcher is asked to deliver a result in two months and is given limited resources for interviewing, transcribing, and analyzing the interviews, then this is obviously very different from a large, well-funded research project that might go on for years and involve hundreds of interviewees. Too many method books are concerned only (or mainly) with ideal research situations, and do not take concrete situations and barriers into account. But some of the most interesting pieces of research seem in fact to have come from non-planned situations that led to small-scale studies, when researchers simply stumbled upon something that emerged as pressing to study (see Brinkmann, 2012a, for examples and discussions of this kind of research).

When dealing with the *how*, the researcher should first and foremost consider whether interviewing is an appropriate way of answering the questions that interest her. Surprisingly, this consideration is often completely by-passed in reported interview research. Ideally, a research report gives the reader a list of reasons that explain why this particular method was the most relevant one to employ. And, if the answer is affirmative, the researcher should decide whether individual interviews or group interviews are preferable. These different forms of interviews were covered in the previous chapter along with the different media that may structure the conversation (face-to-face, telephone, Internet). Suffice it here to say that individual, face-to-face interviews still represent the standard choice in qualitative interviewing, because of the interpersonal contact, context sensitivity, and flexibility that enables interviewers to take advantage of the research logic of qualitative inquiry.

At a more general level, the *how*-question also implies a decision whether to work inductively, deductively, or abductively (or whether to combine these modes). The following section is adapted from Brinkmann, 2012a):

Induction is the process of recording a number of individual instances (e.g. stories about what it means to learn something new) in order to say something general about the given class of instances (e.g. learning). According to traditional formal logic (which is deductive), inductive inference is not strictly valid, for even if the first 99 girls we have observed do in fact "throw like a girl" (cf. Young, 1980), it may be the case that the 100th does not. Nevertheless, qualitative research is most frequently characterized as inductive, since researchers will often enter the field without too many preconceived ideas to test, but will rather let the empirical world decide which specific questions are worth seeking answers to. Grounded theory is one well-known approach that seeks to optimize the inductive process in qualitative inquiry (Glaser & Strauss, 1967). Some methodologists almost identify qualitative research as such with an inductive approach—e.g. Flick (2002, p. 2), who talks about "traditional deductive methodologies," by which he means quantitative research, being superseded by more adequate qualitative "inductive strategies." But as we shall see later in the chapter, it is indeed possible to work deductively in qualitative interviewing, although it demands a different approach to design. Inductive designs are particularly well suited to study new and emergent phenomena, where it is premature to formulate specific hypotheses.

Deduction is a phase in the knowledge-producing process of deducing testable hypotheses from general ideas or theories, and then seeking to falsify these. In philosophy of science, this theory was famously developed as a general approach to the scientific method by Karl Popper and was known as *falsificationism*. The idea was that only those theories that result in hypotheses that are in principle falsifiable deserve to be called scientific. This, according to Popper, excluded Marx and Freud from the rank of scientists. The deductive model may serve the natural sciences well, but is less helpful as a general model in the human and social sciences. The main problem with the deductive approach (and also with falsificationism) is that in cases where empirical observations apparently contradict one's hypothesis or general theory, scientists often will not know whether to reject their hypothesis or ignore their observations (because they are methodologically weak, for example). That said, researchers using qualitative interviewing can work deductively and use single cases as a test bed for general theories, following a deduction of the form "If this is (not) valid for this case, then it applies to all (no) cases." (Flyvbjerg, 2006, p. 230). To give an example: If it turns out that even the most abstract forms of human knowledge—mathematics—are situated and acquired contextually, then we have reason to think that all forms of human knowledge are thus situated (Lave, 1988). By studying an extreme case of something, one may become able to deduce general consequences for the entire class of the given something.

To give a more concrete example of how an interview project can be based on a deductive design, we may mention Kvale's classic (1980) study of the classroom effects of grading. The study arose in connection with a new Danish policy of restricted admission to college based on grade point averages from high school (see also Kvale & Brinkmann, 2008, p. 108). The researchers decided to interview Danish pupils and teachers about their experiences with grading, and they formulated several hypotheses in advance such as (1) Grading influences the process of learning and the social situation where learning occurs, (2) the prevalence of the grading perspective would increase with a restricted admission to college based on grade point averages. These hypotheses were deduced from theories that were prevalent at the time (particularly Marxist ones) about extrinsic motivation for learning in a capitalist society (implying that learning to obtain grades prepares young people to work primarily to obtain an income). Operating with a deductive approach like this demands particular care on behalf of the researchers not to automatically verify the hypotheses (this danger is often referred to as confirmation bias), and, in this case, the research group employed independent coders of the material to ensure high reliability in the interpretations and did many other things to avoid confirmation bias. In any case, this example shows that it is possible to use a deductive model when designing qualitative interview projects, although inductive approaches are much more common.

Both the induction and deduction models normally work best when researchers already know the phenomena that they are studying in the research process (although the deductive model demands much more specificity in this regard). It is tacitly presupposed that we have some stable entity that we can study repeatedly in a number of cases to build general knowledge (induction) or that we already have general ideas from which we can deduce particular consequences to test (deduction). But when we talk about the volatile conversational world of human beings, this is often not the case. Thus, a third kind of reasoning is needed, and fortunately we have what is known as abduction, which is suitable when we wish to study things that are emerging and as yet unknown.

Abduction as a form of reasoning is associated with the pragmatist Charles S. Peirce. Peirce is often credited with being *the* original pragmatist because of his formulation of what has since been known as the "pragmatic maxim": "Consider what effects, which might conceivably have practical bearings, we conceive the objects of our conception to have. Then our conception of these effects is the whole of our conception of the object." (quoted from Bernstein, 2010, p. 3). According to Peirce, things *are* their effects.

Abduction is a form of reasoning that we employ in situations of uncertainty; when we need an understanding or explanation of something that happens or some effect. It can be formalized as follows: (1) We observe X; (2) X is unexpected and breaks with our normal understanding; (3) but if Y is the case, then X makes sense; (4) therefore we are allowed to claim Y, at least provisionally. As an example, let us say (1) that we observe a person who waves her arms wildly. And let us say (2) that this is unexpected in the context (the situation is not, for example, an aerobics class). We can then conjecture (3) that an aggressive wasp is attacking the person. This would make the person's behavior understandable, even expected, and therefore (4) we infer that this is the case (at least until we arrive at a better interpretation).

As this example testifies, abduction is a very pervasive form of reasoning in everyday life. And it is likewise widespread, although more implicitly, in interview studies. In most, if not all, forms of qualitative inquiry, there is an abductive aspect, especially connected to (3), which we may refer to as the creative moment in the analytic process. This is when researchers employ their sociological imagination (Mills, 1959) and develop conjectures about how to understand something, which they then test in practice by looking at evidence for and against (this will be exemplified in Box 2.1, where the researchers develop five different conjectures to explain a given phenomenon). From the abductive angle, research is never finished, as the human world itself is never finished, but constantly in the making. Designing interview studies abductively thus means designing for dialoguing with an evolving reality of persons in conversation rather than attempting to formulate theories that are universally true.

To sum up, it is often relevant for readers of interview reports to know whether the study was conceptualized inductively, deductively, or abductively. An inductive approach demands careful exposition of the theme being investigated and a close description of the steps taken from data generation to formulation of general patterns, types, or ideas in the material. A deductive approach has as its key issue how to design in a way that minimizes the risk of confirmation bias, the tendency to have one's hypotheses confirmed. Finally, with an abductive approach, it becomes imperative to justify and check the interpretive conjectures that are voiced by the researcher. Some studies, of course, successfully combine the different approaches at different stages in the research process (like the study described in Box 2.1 below, when the researcher, Janice Morse, began with an open and inductive approach and, upon discovering a specific phenomenon, developed different hypotheses abductively that were tested in a comparative design with deductive elements).

- *Who* should be interviewed? This is the question of selection and sampling. According to Roulston (who follows LeCompte and Preissle), one needs to draw a distinction between selection and sampling (Roulston, 2010, p. 81). Selection refers to the general decisions concerning who should be in focus in the study (e.g. adults suffering from depression) and sampling refers to the process of finding a subset of the population that has been selected as relevant (e.g. 20 depressed adults, an equal number of women and men, recruited from Clinic X in Y-ville, representing "adults suffering from depression"). In most quantitative studies, the goal is to obtain a representative sample, which may enable researchers to generalize from the sample to the general population. This can also be a goal in qualitative research, but because most qualitative projects aim for thorough analyses in depth—rather than larger and broader analyses—they often employ other sampling strategies.

Sampling becomes a particularly pertinent issue in case-study research, because researchers study just one single case, and Flyvbjerg (2006) discusses a number of different ways of selection, based on different interests.

Random selection can be employed to avoid systematic biases in the sample (here the size of the sample is decisive for generalization, but this is often not relevant for qualitative studies). In general, random selection as a conscious choice is employed only in quantitative projects.

Information-oriented selection is normally more relevant in qualitative inquiry. The goal is here to "maximize the utility of information from small samples and single cases. Cases are selected on the basis of expectations about their information content" (Flyvbjerg, 2006, p. 230). This means that the researcher's knowledge about the field becomes relevant. With information-oriented selection, the researcher can choose to look for (1) *extreme cases* in order to be able to say something about the phenomenon in its purest form (e.g. adults suffering from *severe* depression),

(2) *maximum variation cases* in order to obtain information about the significance of different and perhaps opposing circumstances (e.g. adults with mild versus severe depression), (3) *critical cases* in order to obtain knowledge that allows for deductions and falsifications, which were discussed above (e.g. "if X is found among most people with mild depression, we have reason to believe it will be found among everyone who suffers from depression"), and (4) *paradigmatic cases* that look for the typical in order, as Flyvbjerg says, to "develop a metaphor or establish a school for the domain that the case concerns" (p. 230). Sometimes qualitative interviewers do not have the luxury of choosing a sampling strategy, but must stick to the respondents that they are able to recruit. Like other forms of selection and sampling, the consequences of this should also be reflected upon in the research report.

Regardless of how one ended up with one's groups of participants, the process of selecting, sampling, and recruiting the participants should be described. Readers of interview reports will also expect the researcher to reflect on possible limitations brought to the study because of the actual group of participants. What does it mean if the participants were "self-selected" as volunteers? Does it matter if the researcher accepted "who she could find" as participants, without being able to select among them? Does it matter if the group is skewed in terms of gender, social position, or ethnicity for example?

• *How many* interviews need to be conducted? This is arguably the most typical question raised by interviewers at research courses, but also readers of interview reports will often ask whether the number of people interviewed was sufficiently high (normally they do not ask whether it was sufficiently low, although this question may also be relevant). People frequently ask this question with a quantitative logic in mind: The more interviews, the more valid and reliable the analysis will be. But this is rarely the case. As Kvale has said, the only logical answer to the question "How many interviews should I conduct?" is: "Interview as many subjects as necessary to find out what you need to know." (Kvale & Brinkmann, 2008, p. 113). If the goal of one's study is to find out how it is to be Barack Obama, then it might be sufficient to interview just this one person. If the researcher has given careful thought to how to select interviewees, a small number of interviews may be enough to answer one's research question. If the point is, for example, to test whether a supposed general feature exists in some population, then it might suffice to interview a few critical cases (e.g. those cases where it is least likely to find the feature, and if it is found there, it is likely to be found everywhere).

Normally, fewer interviews that are thoroughly analyzed are preferable to many interviews that are only superficially explored. It is always relevant to bear Harry Wolcott's maxim in mind: "Do less, more thoroughly" (Wolcott, 2009, p. 95). Qualitative interviewing distinguishes itself by its ability to get close to people's lives, not by including a huge number of participants. One cannot get close to the lives of 50 or 100 people in an interview study. If, for some reason, such a large number of participants is needed, a survey would possibly have been better and more economical. And if the study has included 50 participants, but only the voices of a handful of people are reported (which is not unusual), then the reader easily becomes skeptical: What happened to all the other people who were interviewed? Did their words not matter to the researcher? As a rule of thumb, it can be said that interview studies tend to have around 15 participants, which is a number that makes possible a practical handling of the data (although 15 interviews of 20 transcribed pages equals 300 pages to be analyzed, which is quite a bit). The aim is not statistical representativeness (although it can be, e.g. in mixed methods studies), but instead the chance to look in detail at how selected people experience the world.

Interviewing

The preparation phase, with its many considerations about theme and research approach (induction, deduction, abduction), should also include a review of extant literature and normally ends with the creation of an interview guide, which is also sometimes referred to as an interview protocol (Rubin & Rubin, 2012). The guide translates the research questions (e.g. "How do young people in late modernity experience transitions?") into questions that can be posed to interviewees in a language that makes sense to them (e.g. "Could you please describe what happened when you moved away from your parents' house?). Some interviewers prefer a simple list of questions in a specific order, whereas others prefer a page with two columns, one with research themes on one side and another with interview questions that reflect the different themes on the other side. This makes it possible for the interviewer to get an overview of where she is in the conversational process and likely ensures that all relevant themes are covered. It is preferable to memorize the guide as much as possible in order to be able to maintain eye contact with the interviewee. This also facilitates a flexible approach to the order of the questions, and may allow the interviewee to cover something that the interviewer had only expected to touch upon later in the conversation.

Interviewers should think about whether a receptive style or a more assertive style is preferable. For sensitive and personal topics, a supportive, receptive, or responsive approach is often helpful (Rubin & Rubin, 2012). In their introduction to responsive interviewing, Rubin and Rubin emphasize flexibility of design and highlight the interviewer's acceptance of what interviewees say, along with a need for adjusting "to the personalities of both conversational partners." (p. 7). On the other hand, if the goal is to study how people justify their beliefs, deliberate about difficult matters, or give accounts of their opinions, a more confrontational style may be required, which demands particular ethical sensitivity in order to ensure that the conversation is conducted respectfully.

Different styles of interviewing were covered extensively in the previous chapter, and I shall not repeat myself here, but merely emphasize once more that it is preferable to create some sort of alignment between one's research interest, interview style, and the kind of analysis that one expects to carry out. For example, if one's research interest is to capture illness narratives, then it is important to create a corpus of stories from the participants that lend themselves to narrative analysis. It then becomes important to ask interviewees to produce narratives, which can be done quite simply by asking "Could you tell me the story of what happened when you received the diagnosis?" Small linguistic guides (e.g. to "tell the story" instead of "describe the situation" or "reflect upon the meaning of...") often prove to be immensely important when the material is to be analyzed in the next step. Likewise—even if it may sound trivial—if the goal is to analyze the phenomenological essences of particular experiences, then it is pertinent to ask for concrete descriptions; or if the research interest concerns people's account-giving practices, the interviewer should not forget to ask people to give accounts, such as by justifying opinions or answering other why-questions.

Analysis

When the interviews have been conducted, a more focused analytic phase begins. Like the other phases, analysis is not reserved to a post hoc interpretation of transcripts, because the analytic task already begins during the interviews, e.g. when interviewers attempt to understand and interpret what the interviewees are trying to say. It is very common that interviewers summarize a narrative or description and ask the participant for verification or further reflections. This was the fourth element in the conversational flow illustrated in Box 1.1 in the previous chapter. Doing this is, in a rather simple way, already beginning to analyze the statements by trying to achieve a form of interviewee validation *in situ*.

Also, the process of transcribing the recorded conversations should be thought of as part of the analysis. Transcribing necessarily means translating from one medium (the spoken word) to another (the written word), and researchers should think about how they are going to transcribe early on in the process. Many different approaches to transcription exist. These include very detailed conversation analytic approaches such as Gail Jefferson's, which demands the marking of overlap between speakers, emphasis, volume, delay, and so on, and which is very time-consuming; verbatim transcriptions that may include laughter, hmms, and breaks; and reconstructive transcriptions that "polish" and provide order to the often messy utterances of the speakers. There is no golden standard of transcription. Everything depends on the purpose of one's investigation and on what is possible in practice (what resources in terms of time or salary for assistants are available). But it is obvious that if one's analysis concerns the fine machinery of turn-taking, or how the form of speech shapes the meaning of what is said, then there is a need to transcribe the finer details of talk, whereas a more rough transcription might be in order if the purpose is to study the life stories of the participants. In any case, to transcribe is always to analyze in the original sense of analysis (literally "to break down into units").

Not all researchers transcribe the entire empirical corpus. Some prefer to work directly with the sound recording, which can be coded in most contemporary software programs for qualitative analysis, and some transcribe only selected portions of the corpus. After transcription, a more focused analysis of the material can be carried out, and here the options are legion and depend on the philosophical and theoretical position of the researcher and obviously also on the purpose of the study. Again, we may use the distinction between inductive, deductive, and abductive strategies to describe three broad approaches to analysis:

Induction in its different varieties is the most widespread approach to analysis. Some qualitative researchers talk about analysis as "analytic induction," which, in the broadest sense, refers to "the systematic examination of similarities within and across cases to develop concepts, ideas, or theories." (Pascale, 2011, p. 53). Analysts using this strategy will inductively code data to identify patterns and formulate potential explanations of these patterns. So, a key component of analytic induction is coding. Coding can be either concept-driven or data-driven. Concept-driven coding uses codes that have been developed in advance by the researcher, either by looking at selected portions of the material or by consulting the existing literature. Data-driven coding implies that the researcher starts out without codes, and develops them upon reading the material. In principle, anything can be coded depending on the research interest. Gibbs (2007) suggests the following examples: particular acts, events, activities, strategies, states, meanings, norms, symbols, level of participation, relationships, conditions or constraints, consequences, settings. Also reflexive codings can be used that record the researcher's role in the process (pp. 47–48).

Coding also plays a significant role in the inductive methodology known as *grounded theory*, originally developed by Glaser and Strauss (1967). Grounded theory is an inductive strategy for theory development without a prior theoretical framework. Many grounded theorists work with open coding in a process of "breaking down, examining, comparing, conceptualizing and categorizing data" (Strauss & Corbin, 1990, p. 61). Grounded theories are developed through the use of conceptualization to bind facts together, rather than through inferences and deductive hypothesis testing. Since the creation of grounded theory in the 1960s, it has branched in many different directions, including the more constructivist position represented by Charmaz (2011) and the postmodern variant known as situational analysis, developed by Clarke (2005). Charmaz makes clear that grounded theory is inductive at its core and will proceed with analysis by comparing data with data (developing codes), comparing data and codes (developing tentative categories), and developing categories into overarching concepts that are compared with (other) theoretical concepts. These are, roughly, the analytic stages recommended in grounded theory. But Charmaz notes that grounded theory also has an *abductive* component since it highlights the importance of being *surprised* in the development of codes, categories, and theoretical concepts. So, as always in qualitative inquiry, it can be fruitful to mix the different analytic strategies.

A final example of an inductive approach to analysis is empirical phenomenology, which may serve as an example of *experience-focused analysis*, because of its ambition to study the essential structures of conscious experience. Phenomenology sometimes applies inductive analysis as a kind of *meaning condensation* (Kvale & Brinkmann, 2008, p. 205). This refers to an abridgement of the meanings articulated by the research participants into briefer formulations. Longer utterances are condensed into shorter statements in which the main sense of what is said is rephrased in a few words. This technique rests on the idea in phenomenology that there is a certain essential structure to the way we experience things in the life world (see the previous chapter), which is what constitutes an experience *as* an experience of a given something (shame, anxiety, love, learning something new etc.).

An even more specific approach to phenomenological analysis has been developed in a psychological context by Amedeo Giorgi (e.g. Giorgi & Giorgi, 2003). Giorgi breaks the analytic process down into four steps: (1) Obtain a concrete description of a phenomenon (through an interview) as lived through by someone. Read the description carefully and become familiar with it to get a sense of the whole. (2) Establish meaning units in the description. (3) Transform each meaning unit into expressions that communicate the psychological sense of the data. (4) Based upon the transformed meaning units, articulate the general structure of the experience of the phenomenon (p. 170).

While grounded theory is an analytic technique that is relatively independent of specific theoretical perspectives on human life and experience, phenomenology is in a way a complete package of theory, philosophy of science, and methodology (see e.g. Langdridge, 2007). The advantage of using such a "package" is that peers will know what to expect from an analysis since there is much agreement concerning which questions to pose in an analysis as a researcher (and *to* the analysis, if one is the reader of it). The disadvantage is the rather constricted and standardized format, which may limit the creative development of qualitative analyses. Today, many qualitative researchers prefer to move freely between different methods of analysis. This, however, usually demands a more careful description of their analytic procedures so that readers have a chance to evaluate the validity of the possible idiosyncratic work.

Deduction in the analytic phase can involve the use of hypotheses derived from theory in an interpretive process. In Box 2.1, we shall soon see an example of how hypotheses can also be derived from the empirical material itself and tested in a comparative analysis. Herbert Blumer once referred to theoretical concepts as *sensitizing instruments* that researchers use as tools to be able to look in fruitful directions and helpful ways (see Clarke, 2005, p. 28). Some qualitative researchers, e.g. those working on the basis of philosophical hermeneutics (Gadamer, 1960), believe that we cannot understand anything without prejudices in the literal sense of pre-judgments. There is no such thing as understanding something from nowhere, without presuppositions, for we always need some interpretive framework in order to distinguish significant from insignificant aspects of the material. Some of these frameworks can be formulated explicitly as theories. Psychoanalysis is one such famous theory that enabled its practitioners and theorists to see and understand something that was not visible without the sensitizing concepts of psychoanalysis (e.g. repression, defense mechanisms, Oedipus complex, etc.). On a less paradigmatic level, many researchers today approach their empirical material analytically with theoretical concepts drawn from narrative theory (e.g. story line, plot, protagonist, antagonist, etc.). In both cases, it is possible to deduce hypotheses from general theories that can assist in the analytic process of reading and interpreting the data.

This kind of deductive analytic strategy is very often criticized for its confirmation bias, which I also discussed above. Critics argue that analysts will find whatever the theory posits. This, however, is hardly an issue that is unique to qualitative research, but can be said to be a universal human tendency. Fortunately, a number of strategies exist to counter this tendency, e.g. to play the devil's advocate against one's own interpretations. If this is done sincerely, rather than just as window-dressing, it can lead to new and exciting perspectives on the materials. Flyvbjerg (2006) cites a number of social scientists who have argued that qualitative case studies may often lead to a refining of preexisting theory or even to discarding general theories that turn out not to hold when confronted with empirical realities. Flyvbjerg refers to this as case studies functioning like "black swans," borrowing the well-known example from logic that general statements (such as "all swans are white") can be falsified just by finding a single instance that contradicts them (e.g. by finding a species of black swans in Australia). If the analyst meticulously shows the reader that care has been taken to avoid confirmation bias, then the ensuing text may become very persuasive, and it often results in a highly readable product if the researcher constructs the text like a series of challenges to her own interpretations that are discussed in turn. A further sign of quality is seen when researchers present several different interpretations of the phenomenon under scrutiny rather than just sticking to a single one. This can be achieved by working with more than one theoretical framework, leading to different sets of "sensitizing concepts" that may bring forth different aspects of the material in the analytic process.

Abduction in the analytic phase works from breakdowns in the understanding of the analyst. The researcher will look for breaks and contradictions and other matters that somehow "disturb" the common understanding or convention. Some interview researchers, who work abductively in a broad sense, look in particular at the social practice of interviewing itself as the key to open up for analysis. Roulston (2011) has argued that there is much to learn from "failed" interviews, i.e., from interviews where things "go wrong" according to textbooks on interviewing and conventional wisdom. In Table 1.1 from the previous chapter, which drew a distinction between two conceptions of interviewing—as a research instrument and as a social practice—we can say that Roulston encourages interviewers to pay close attention to the nature of the conversational interaction itself and to look for misunderstandings or other breaks in the conversational flow. Aspects that stand out as strange may often prove to be valuable to understanding how talking about the subject matter in a specific way constructs what we may know about it.

As one example of this, we may mention Tanggaard (2007), who did a research project on learning in a vocational school and conducted many interviews with students. The researcher conceived of learning as embedded in everyday activities, whereas it was made clear from interviews with vocational students that learning—according to the learners' perspective—was something that took place in a school. According to Tanggaard, this led to "discourses crossing swords" in the interviews, implying a struggle about how to define learning. The interviews did not appear as smooth and responsive, but rather as full of breaks, misunderstandings, and even antagonisms. This was made clear to Tanggaard only upon reading the transcripts and employing what I here have called abductive reasoning. It was her readings of Foucault's theory in particular that enabled the articulation of ideas about how to make sense of the struggle of the conversationalists. In her study, the opposition between the speakers—interviewer and interviewee—made it clear that "learning" is not a simple thing, but is a multi-perspectival phenomenon. The "what" of the conversation (the subject matter) cannot here be separated from the "how" of the situated interaction of interviewing.

Thus, unlike analytic induction, thematic analysis, grounded theory, and phenomenology—all of which aim to capture the lived experience as reported in interviews—analyses that look at interviews from an abductive angle in this sense will more often be discourse-focused and will treat interview data as topics (rather than resources) and analyze them as accounts occasioned by the situation (rather than reports about past experience). Needless to say, it is often helpful for readers of interview reports to learn how the analysts have treated the data in the process of analysis: as accounts, as reports, or both.

Reporting

The final step of an interview project is the reporting of the results. Like with the other steps, reporting cannot be treated as a discrete stage, but is in its own way important throughout the process. Ideally, interviewers should proceed with preparations, interviews, and analyses with the final end product—the report—in mind. For qualitative research, it is the case that analysis and reporting in particular often melt together. Writing is "a method of inquiry" (Richardson & St.Pierre, 2005) throughout an interview study. Writing is a central way for qualitative researchers not just to report some findings, in the final instance, but also to experiment with analyses, compare different perspectives on the empirical material, and try out a number of alternative ways of presenting readings of the material. Writing should therefore be treated as an intrinsic part of the methodology of interview research and not as a final "postscript" added on at the end.

Since reporting is treated in great detail in the following chapters on writing up the methods section and writing up the research findings, I shall leave it here and encourage the reader to continue reading! The most important thing to bear in mind in relation to design questions is that the well designed project reflects on how to report at the outset. If the goal is to write a single short article, care should be taken not to obtain too much material to analyze, but if the goal is to write a long and thorough book, matters are very different. One should never ignore such practicalities, since the form of a good report supports the content of what the researcher is trying to say.

Designing for Discovering, Constructing or Understanding?

The four stages of *preparation, interviewing, analysis,* and *reporting* are characteristic of most interview projects across subject matters and theoretical paradigms. The underlying goals and research interests of different projects may, however, be quite different. I shall here reduce the many possible research interests to just three and provide an example of each. I will invoke a distinction, which initially looks rather abstract and philosophical, but which may have quite concrete implications for the research process. For although there is no direct coupling between kinds of design on the one hand and research interests on the other, it is often the case that tight, preset designs are meant to maximize the chances for the researcher *discovering* hitherto unknown features of reality, whereas more flexible designs are meant to facilitate the researcher's better *understanding* of something. In addition, it is also possible to design in a way that involves *constructing* something new. In short, qualitative interview researchers should know (and communicate to their readers) whether they are trying to:

- *Discover* something that they do not know.
- *Construct* something that they (or their requestors) would like to see happen.
- *Understand* something that they do not understand.

Concerning the relation between research design and research interest, we may refer to the great hermeneutic philosopher Gadamer (1960), who argued that the process of understanding something cannot be codified into methodological rules to be specified prior to the research process. In order to make sense of Gadamer's argument, you may ask yourself the following: What methods do you use when reading, and hopefully understanding, this book? What methods do you use when you try to understand the people you meet and talk to? In general, according to hermeneutic scholars, we do *not* employ methods in such cases, and it is misguided when some qualitative methodologists pretend that certain methodological procedures will guarantee good and insightful research by themselves. What we do in order to understand people (a primary aim for qualitative researchers) is spend time with them and talk to them. So, from a hermeneutic angle, it will sometimes be the case that a strict design, based on formal and standardized methodological rules, will not be helpful when understanding is the aim. This, however, should not lead us to discard design questions. Hermeneutically oriented interview research is also designed (albeit not necessarily in a methodologically strict manner), and hermeneutic interviewers, inspired by Gadamer, should nonetheless think through the steps of an interview project as outlined above.

In a recent book, Martin Hammersley (2011) discusses the three different models of research: The discovery model, the construction model, and the hermeneutic or understanding model. They correspond to three different research interests. The discovery model is probably closest to people's intuitive ideas about scientific research: Its rationale is to discover something new; just as physiologists have discovered the functions of organs and astronomers have discovered new planets and stars. In 20th century philosophy of science, however, the discovery model gradually fell out of fashion, because arguments were voiced (e.g. from the aforementioned Gadamer) to the effect that human and social science phenomena are not independent of researchers in a straightforward manner. What we "see," in qualitative research, are historical and cultural phenomena (e.g. patterns of feeling, thinking, talking, and acting) that are constituted by human activities (discourses, symbolic interactions, etc.), including the very activity of gaining knowledge about them. So, the argument went, it is misleading to say that we "discover" them, for we always already have some kind of implicit knowledge about them.

Even in light of such arguments, I believe that it is premature to discard the discovery model. Even if there are valid philosophical reasons to claim that the phenomena studied by qualitative researchers are not independent of human activity (a claim I agree with), I still believe that it makes sense to say—in a more everyday sense of the term—that researchers can discover aspects of these phenomena. They can, as Noblit and Hare (1988) once expressed it, "make the obvious obvious" for us, and thereby discover something that might have been there all along in our lives, but remained unnoticed, perhaps due to its very pervasiveness. I have argued elsewhere (Brinkmann, 2012a) that phenomenological approaches are particularly adept at making the obvious obvious, and Iris Marion Young's paper "Throwing like a girl" is one of my favorite examples of what wonderful and enlightening descriptions of the mundane may result from using this strategy (Young, 1980). In the paper, Young shows how boys and girls learn to move their bodies in quite different ways, which cannot be accounted for in terms of anatomical differences, but concerns socialization. When reading her analysis, one is likely to react with a feeling of recognition; she describes something we knew all along, but which we did not know *that* we knew!

For interview projects that aim for discovery, it is very important to design the study in a way that allows the phenomena to appear in a way that is not controlled by, or a simple artifact of, the researcher's actions. To paraphrase the words of sociologist of science, Bruno Latour (2000), one must make sure to "allow the objects to object" to what researchers say about them and do to them. Only in that way can we attain a level of objectivity that allows for genuine discoveries. In other words, one must discipline the researcher's activities, and this is done most directly by methodology that may make the research procedures more transparent to readers. Below, in Box 2.1, I shall present an example of an interview study that discovered something new about the human world, which was facilitated by a careful methodological design.

Box 2.1 **Discovery Through Qualitative Interviewing**

....

When preparing and researching for this book, I sent e-mails to leading scholars in the field of qualitative interviewing, asking for exemplars of excellent interview projects and publications. In her kind reply, Janice Morse directed my attention to a study of burn patients who had experienced agonizing injuries (Morse & Mitcham, 1998). Morse is the founder of the International Institute for Qualitative Methodology at the University of Alberta, which is a leading qualitative research institution in North America, and she has also founded the journals *Qualitative Health Research* and the *International Journal of Qualitative Methods*. She has thus been a very central figure in qualitative research for decades, in particular qualitative health research, and is extremely experienced as reviewer, editor, and author of papers based on qualitative interviewing.

The study was done by Morse herself together with a colleague, and in her e-mail she explains why she believes it is important. She describes an interesting process of analyzing the data that eventually led to the published paper. In the process, she almost stumbled upon the key to unlock the structure of the data and thereby of the phenomenon: "While analyzing I walked away from my computer, and when I came back I glanced at the screen and had a wow moment suddenly noticing how disjointed the text was. Everyday language took on a new meaning." (E-mail, August 30, 2011). "The text," referred to by Morse, is the textual material from the participants' statements. She continues: "I worked from this single observation to other data sets, 'testing hypotheses' with the already collected data. The moral of this story is that when you hear the interview in the interview setting, that is one level of analysis. Another may unfold when you work with the text."

The study illustrates that qualitative interviewing can lead to genuine *discoveries*. In this case, the discovery was about the language use of patients with catastrophic burn injuries. The primary research question concerned how such patients "get through" the experience and cope with "resulting disabilities, losses of body integrity, alterations in their former sense of self, and often the death of other family members involved in the same accident." (Morse & Mitcham, 1998, p. 667).

One aspect of coping with the agonizing physical pain identified in the literature is *disembodiment*, a distinct distancing from one's own body. And, as Morse recounts, when analyzing the interview statements of the patients, she discovered that they regularly referred to parts of themselves as objects, using "it," "the," and "this" (e.g. talking about "the left hand" rather than "my left hand"). In order to interpret this peculiar use of language, which she had not been aware of in the course of interviewing the participants, but only noticed as in a flash on the computer screen, the researchers compared the language use of burn patients with that of patients with experiences of pain that stem from other kinds of injuries (e.g., spinal cord injuries). They found that other groups of patients (which would be called "control groups" in quantitative research designs) use disembodying language to a much lesser extent, if at all.

Methodologically, the interviewers used narrative analysis of relatively unstructured, but focused, interviews to identify the phenomenon. Initially, Morse took a phenomenological attitude and displayed an interest in just letting the patients "tell their stories" (Morse & Mitcham, 1998, p. 668). But, in a subsequent analytic stage, and upon discovering the particular use of disembodying language, she went beyond phenomenological description to develop hypotheses (or "conjectures," as they are called in the paper), based on the patient narratives, to account for their language use. This represents a deductive phase in the research process, leading to five different hypotheses (ranging from disembodiment being caused by loss of sensation, by loss of physical ability, as something learned from physicians, as a means to protect the self, and finally as a means of controlling overwhelming pain). Out of the five different hypotheses, the researchers found evidence only for the fifth and final one: Disembodiment is a strategy used to remove the body part in order to remove the pain, when it is overwhelming (p. 671). Furthermore, the researchers found that later in the patients' rehabilitation period, patients again go back to using possessive pronouns when referring to the self.

Unlike many other interview studies that claim to have identified some novel phenomenon, the researchers in this case distinguish themselves by also looking at negative cases, i.e. examples of interviews when patients do *not* use disembodying language. This definitely adds to the credibility of the findings, since one gets a sense of researcher trustworthiness as a reader, and, as the researchers explain, there is no reason to think that a negative case invalidates a more general observation (Morse & Mitcham, 1998, p. 670).

All in all, we can say that the study conducted and reported by Morse and Mitcham was designed in a way that enabled a genuine *discovery*. There is generally no formula for how to discover something new, and, as Morse recounts in her e-mail, it simply struck her when looking at the computer screen that there was something peculiar about the interviewee's statements. Unlike other designs that aim to construct a new kind of process, or understand something that one has already identified, this study shows that qualitative interviewing can lead to discoveries, even if the number of participants included is relatively small (initially, six patients with burn injuries were interviewed). The study further illustrates that it is possible, and in this case desirable, to work with a form of deduction in the analytic stage, i.e. qualitative "hypothesis testing." Conjectures about how to explain the phenomenon were deduced from the material and tested in a process that involved comparisons with the experiences and language use of other relevant patient groups.

The next models of research discussed by Hammersley are the construction and understanding models. In a practical down-to-earth sense, the construction model builds on the idea that the goal of qualitative research often is to create something new, e.g. a new or improved social practice, or even new kinds of people who have changed and developed as a consequence of taking part in a qualitative study. In Chapter 1, this was presented as the transformative model of interviewing. Qualitative interviewers are increasingly becoming aware that interviewing, as Briggs (2003, p. 497) has argued, is "a 'technology' that invents both notions of individual subjectivities and collective social and political patterns." Different conversational practices, including research interviews, produce and activate different forms of subjectivity, and, utilizing some of the more activist forms of interviewing discussed in the previous chapter, one goal of interviewing can be to construct subjects in ways that allow for new kinds of action.

In a more abstract epistemological sense, the construction model is in many ways a direct answer to the perceived problems of the discovery model. Scholars subscribing to the construction model (e.g. Gergen, 2001, and other so-called social constructionists) argue that knowledge is always constructed rather than discovered, and that we can never know what or how things are in separation from human activities. There are no "things in themselves," but only "things constructed by us." In its strong form, as Hammersley critically points out, social constructionism seems to undermine the very possibility of knowledge, because the only conception of knowledge available (to strong constructionists) is one that presents knowledge as what most people believe. This conflates knowledge and belief, and ignores the everyday necessity of distinguishing between what *is* true and what it *taken* to be true (Hammersley, 2011, p. 131). It also leads to the unhappy consequence that a powerful group of people can create truths by persuading or forcing others to believe certain things that are in the interest of the powerful group. Furthermore, in its strong form, constructionism leads to the consequence that most questions about research design can be ignored, because all knowledge is seen as a unique function of the steps taken to obtain it. In its weaker forms, the construction model fades into the understanding model, albeit with a greater emphasis on the fact that qualitative inquiry is meant to change aspects of the social world. An example of this is given below in Box 2.2.

Box 2.2 Constructing Through Qualitative Interviewing

One of the interview studies that I keep returning to is the classic reported in *Habits of the Heart: Individualism and Commitment in American Life* by sociologists Bellah, Madsen, Sullivan, Swidler, and Tipton (1985). The empirical material for this study of North American character and values consisted of interviews with more than 200 participants, some of whom were interviewed more than once. In an insightful appendix to the book, the authors present their philosophy of science as "social science as public philosophy." They reject the common view of the social science as "a disembodied cognitive enterprise" (p. 301), and advocate instead a dialogical role of the social sciences in which research functions to raise important questions about values for society. In this way, the book aimed not simply to represent aspects of US culture to its readers, but to construct a discussion about where the United States are going as a society.

In order to achieve this, the researchers conducted a special kind of interview, which they refer to as "active interviews" (Bellah, Madsen, Sullivan, Swidler & Tipton, 1985). Active interviews correspond quite closely to the Socratic interviews that I introduced earlier in this book (see the previous chapter). In contrast to the interviewer as a friend or therapist, probing deep in the private psyche of the interviewee, the active interviews were intended to generate public conversation about societal values and goals. Such active interviews did not necessarily aim for agreement between interviewer and interviewee, and the interviewer was allowed to question and challenge what the interviewee said. In one of the examples cited, the interviewer, Ann Swidler, was trying to get the respondent to clarify the basis of his moral judgments crystallized in his statement that "lying is one of the things I want to regulate"—and Swidler asked him why:

A: Well, it's a kind of thing that is a habit you get into. Kind of self-perpetuating. It's like digging a hole. You just keep digging and digging.

Q: So why is it wrong?

A: Why is integrity important and lying bad? I don't know. It just is. It's just so basic. I don't want to be bothered with challenging that. It's part of me. I don't know where it came from, but it's very important.

Q: When you think about what's right and what's wrong, are things bad because they are bad for people, or are they right and wrong in themselves, and if so how do you know?

A: Well some things are bad because... I guess I feel like everybody on this planet is entitled to have a little bit of space, and things that detract from other people's space are kind of bad... (Bellah, Madsen, Sullivan, Swidler & Tipton, 1985, pp. 304–305)

Swidler challenges the respondent to examine why lying is wrong, which is quite a hard philosophical question, and the final question cited—concerning why wrong things are wrong—seems very complex, and in standard textbooks on interviewing, the question could appear as an example of how *not* to pose an interview question. The question is (extremely) abstract and invites high conceptual reflection rather than concrete description. It very much resembles Socrates' questions in Plato's dialogues.

The methodological appendix can be read as a very honest and straightforward account of how a qualitative research group has worked. There are no details about the specific analytical steps, but a rich description of the discussions that the researchers had, how they interviewed, and the kinds of philosophical literature that inspired them. This is quite typical of studies that are designed to construct a discussion, in this case of the question that is the opening sentence of the book, "How ought we to live?" (Bellah, Madsen, Sullivan, Swidler & Tipton, 1985, p. vii).

The study by Bellah and co-workers does not represent a strong form of social constructionism, but rather a view of social inquiry as already a part of the society it studies. There is no place outside society from which to obtain an objective view of social processes, so qualitative social science must instead seek to construct a better social world by initiating discussions about society and its problems. Bellah's study also has great affinities with what Hammersley calls the understanding model (which is actually the one favored by Hammersley himself), and this is what I will focus on now.

The understanding model agrees with the critics of the discovery model that there is no knowledge whose validity is simply given (Hammersley, 2011, p. 132). But it simultaneously goes against the radical constructionist conclusion that this implies that knowledge can be constructed freely by human beings. We are constrained, as Gadamer would say, by the historical horizon of our interpretations, by the inescapable framework provided by culture and history that constitutes our world. We understand reality from where we stand, but there are still more and less accurate, fruitful, and, valid ways of understanding from where we are. So, in that sense, the understanding model assumes that knowledge can be both perspectival and objective at the same time, and it also implies that we cannot freely choose where to stand. We are situated somewhere in the conversational world (cf. Chapter 1), and that should not be seen as a hindrance to objective knowledge, but as a precondition of it.

When working from the understanding model, qualitative interviewers must design their research projects in a way that enables what Gadamer called a "fusion of horizons" that leads neither to a forgetting of one's own perspective, nor to totalizing the other that one seeks to understand. As the moral philosopher and phenomenologist Lévinas would say, the goal, which is at once ethical and epistemological, is to avoid the main ill of Western philosophy, viz. the reduction of the other to the same (Levinas, 1969). One should respect, and perhaps even celebrate, difference, and yet try to understand it. Interviewers, who use conversations to understand the lives of others, must therefore reflect upon how their own background (standpoints, methodologies etc.) affects their understanding, but they should not say (like some constructionists) that this background *determines* what they see.

Before summing up and concluding on design issues in qualitative interviewing, I shall present an interview study that is quite different from the ones presented in Box 2.1 and Box 2.2, and which rested on a different kind of design. Although not articulated in exactly these terms, the example presented in Box 2.3 is of an interview study which, I believe, nicely illustrates a kind of fusion of horizons, which was enabled by a very flexible design.

Box 2.3 **Understanding Through Qualitative Interviewing**

My attention was directed to the study described here by Martin Packer, author of *The Science of Qualitative Research* (Packer, 2011) and editor of the journal *Qualitative Research in Psychology*, when I asked him about examples of excellent interview studies. Packer gave the following kind answer in an e-mail:

> "I have not been looking out especially for good examples of research interviewing, but one example that comes to mind is Loïc Wacquant's article "The pugilistic point of view: How boxers think and feel about their trade" (Wacquant, 1995). This is part of a larger study, and Wacquant has published almost a dozen articles and a book. But this one focuses on his interviews with boxers. I think there are some contradictions in it (for example, I don't believe that the boxers forgot

he was a teacher), but he manages to convince me that he is reconstructing an embedded and embodied form of understanding." (E-mail, August 18, 2011).

Upon reading Wacquant's analysis, I must agree with Packer's verdict. The article indeed communicates an embedded and embodied form of understanding. It does not, perhaps, report on any new *discoveries*, nor was the study conducted to *construct* changes in specific social practices, but it nicely illustrates how qualitative interviewing can be designed for *understanding* and why this may be a valuable thing to aim for.

Wacquant is a sociologist, born in France, who is working at the University of Califonia, Berkeley. He collaborated closely with the famous sociologist Pierre Bourdieu, and is an editor and co-founder of the journal *Ethnography*. In his article here, he describes and reconstructs the boxer's point of view (which he calls the pugilistic point of view, referring to boxing as pugilism). From August 1988 until October 1991, Wacquant conducted participant observation at a boxing gym in Chicago (on its South Side). He was here educated in the art of boxing, and his career as a boxer culminated with a fight at Chicago's Golden Gloves tournament (which, alas, he lost).

Like Bourdieu, Wacquant wishes to develop a "carnal sociology" that is not just a sociology of talking or observing selves, but one that involves embodied people, situated in social practices. Understanding the lives of people, from this "carnal" point of view implies living a life that approximates that of the people one wants to understand. In relation to interviewing boxers, it involves "taking seriously what ordinary boxers have to say about their occupation: how they think and feel about this harsh trade to which they are willing to give so much, what virtues it holds for them, and how it affects their life and self." (Wacquant, 1995, p. 490). Wacquant thus acts as a qualitative interviewer as an inherent aspect of learning the craft of boxing and talking to his fellow apprentices. He wants to obtain a view at prizefighting from the "inside looking out" (p. 490).

In the paper, Wacquant draws upon in-depth semi-structured interviews with 50 fighters, comprising, he says, almost all professional fighters in Illinois in 1991, and, in the course of the research process, he ended up with 2,000 pages of transcriptions (Wacquant, 1995, p. 493). Because he had been in the community for almost three years before the formal interviews were conducted, he was able to "phrase [his] questions in a manner congruent with their occupational concerns and thus elicit candid and meaningful answers" (p. 490). Unlike the majority of today's interview studies, which involve participants with whom the interviewer just meets for an hour or so, Wacquant had prepared extremely well by spending numerous hours, weeks, and even years with the participants. So the interviews "were not the product of a fleeting and superficial encounter but one link in an extended chain of routine interpersonal exchanges." (p. 494).

Wacquant's article is full of detailed analyses of boxers, their lives and practice, and is informed by an understanding of the social situation of the boxers, most of whom "reside in segregated and degraded neighborhoods where violent crime is a basic fact of everyday life and where physical insecurity infests all spheres of existence." (Wacquant, 1995, p. 497). There is thus a combination of a macrosociological angle and minute analyses of the skilled bodily trade of boxing—the *kinetic technique* as he calls it (p. 504)—and there is first and foremost an acknowledgement of and respect for the fact that boxing can infuse the lives of boxers "with a sense of value, excitement, and accomplishment." (p. 501). As one of the boxers, Henri (a black light-heavyweight) said: "It's a *thinkin' man's game*, but the outside doesn't see that. The on'y thin' they see is jus' two guys throwin' punches, you know. Well, uh, you gotta think about *what* you gonna do, *when* you gonna do it, and *how* you gonna do it. See, this is what you gotta think about." (p. 503).

Toward the end of the article, Wacquant expresses his writing ambition: to outline "a picture of the pugilistic planet as its main inhabitants see it, or like to imagine it." (Wacquant, 1995, p. 519). He admits that the account is rather one-sided in its emphasis on the virtues of prizefighting, but a certain ambivalence also creeps in, e.g. when the interviewee Danny talks about his attitude to his son's boxing: "No, no, *no fighter wants their son* [to box], I mean you could hear it, you hear it even in [Jack] Dempsey's age: you never want your son to fight—*that's the reason why you fight, so he won't be able to fight...* It's too hard, it's jus' too damn hard." (p. 523).

In concluding on Wacquant's study, we can say that his interviews with the boxers reported in this article and elsewhere were parts of a larger and longer-lasting ethnographic project of understanding the world of boxing from the inside. The project was thus designed for understanding something that many people do not understand, and even look upon with contempt. Regardless of one's pre-understanding of boxing, I doubt that anyone can maintain a simplistic view of boxing after having read Wacquant's descriptions. He has used his conversations with the boxers, aided by his own life as an apprentice of the craft, to understand their world—and his paper communicates this understanding in an artful way to the readers.

With such an interview study, we are at the most flexible and iterative end of the design continuum. The point is not that this is a sloppy design, without prior specification of the number of interviewees and preparation of an interview guide, but rather that it is the most adequate kind of design when one is aiming at this form of understanding.

The philosophical remarks that I introduced above, about different models of qualitative research designs, should not be taken to imply that qualitative interviewers ought to become philosophers (although a dose of philosophical reflection would rarely hurt). However, it would be helpful if they lived up to a minimal philosophical requirement, viz. to think through and make explicit what kind of model (or combination of models) their design rests on. Only if researchers do so can others evaluate whether the study is theoretically coherent and designed in a way that makes its goal realistic. It is certainly possible to work eclectically and combine research tools from different models, but many interview studies simply proceed with what looks like a phenomenological design of the interviewing process (searching for essential structures of human experience), combined with an oath to the philosophy of social constructionism that denies reality to all essential structures of experience. This is unreflective and illegitimate (and contradictory) eclecticism that makes interpretations of the findings very difficult.

Conclusions

In this chapter, I have introduced a number of theoretical distinctions that enable us to conceptualize different kinds of design. I introduced a generic step-wise model that is good to keep in mind when considering the design of qualitative interview studies, involving the steps of preparation, interviewing, analysis, and reporting, and I outlined three broad aims for qualitative interviewing: Discovery, construction, and understanding. There are many questions about design that are common regardless of the aim of the research project—which I conceptualized as the *what*, the *why*, the *how*, the *who*, and the *how many*—but there are also some issues that relate more specifically to each of the three broad aims.

Researchers aiming for discovery need to design their project in such a way that they minimize the risk that what they discover is simply an artifact of the study itself. This can be achieved by thinking carefully about the way that the interviewing is conducted, including an awareness of possible effects of leading questions, and also by striving for high validity and reliability when transcribing, coding, and analyzing the materials.

Researchers aiming for construction need a particular ethical sensitivity about the way that they expect the world to change in response to their research endeavors. Not all interviewees have an interest in changing when taking part in a study, and not all communities have asked for social change. Furthermore, researchers need to account for why the research is of value when it is not primarily an epistemic affair, seeking truth or understanding.

Finally, researchers aiming for understanding, who often need to work with a more flexible design and to constantly accommodate to the vagaries of the field they are studying, need to think about how they can document the different twists and turns that their research project undergoes. If Gadamer is correct that understanding is non-methodical, then they cannot rely on methodological specifications but must find other, more descriptive ways, of capturing and justifying the knowledge-producing process.

I also introduced three models of reasoning in qualitative research, viz. induction, deduction, and abduction. Roughly, these models correspond to designs that are data-driven, theory-driven, and breakdown-driven (this will be explained more fully in the next chapter). I tried to show how these models may play a role when designing a qualitative interview project, and also that they have particular significance in the analytic phase of research. Three examples were brought in: Janice Morse's study of burn patients, Robert Bellah and colleagues' study of North American values, and Loïc Wacquant's study of boxers.

The first example demonstrated how to design in a way that makes possible the discovery of something new. One may design an interview study in such a way that the chances for discovery are optimized, but the discovery itself will often happen—as described by Morse—more as something for which one cannot plan. Morse's study also shows how different models of reasoning may enter a project in different phases: At first, on my reading, the project was largely inductive, before Morse stumbled upon something interesting and surprising, which led to an abductive formulation of conjectures that were then tested deductively in a comparative design that involved other groups of patients.

The second example illustrates the possibility of designing for construction, viz. the construction of public debate about the future direction of an individualist society, about which the research group was concerned.

Finally, Wacquant's study exemplified a study that was designed for understanding. Obviously, one can also say that there was an element of discovery in the study (uncovering hidden aspects of the lives of boxers) and also of construction (since he was interested in constructing a more positive story about boxing as a lifestyle), and there are not sharp boundaries between these three aims of research. Still, it makes sense to say that the point of the study for Wacquant was to understand the practices of boxing by immersing himself in it. In order to do so, he had to acquire the bodily skills and master the discourse of boxers. This did facilitate a fascinating form of understanding from the inside that he was able to communicate to his readers. Concerning the inductive, deductive, and abductive strategies it seems fair to say that Wacquant's study was mainly inductive, designed without prior hypotheses to be tested, but based on a willingness to learn and gradually get deeper into the field of interest.

3

WRITING UP THE METHODS SECTION

THIS CHAPTER is about how to write up the methodological procedures of an interview study. The most general rule across paradigmatic differences is: Describe what you have done and why. Qualitative research interviewing is a craft in which much is tacit and based on skills rather than unambiguous steps that can be followed more or less mechanically. A significant function of a methods section is to make explicit and transparent what is often done unreflectively by skilled researchers, so that readers may look over the researcher's shoulder. In qualitative interviewing, the researcher herself is the most important instrument for producing knowledge, and part of a good methods section addresses this "instrument" and what role it has played in the knowledge-producing process. Other parts of the methods section can be more "mechanical," e.g. concerning transcription rules, etc.

I will touch upon both standard formats for writing-up methodological procedures and non-traditional formats in which methodological descriptions are often integrated into the more general narrative of the text. Different genres are suitable for different purposes, so instead of devising universal rules for how to do it, I will include some examples that illustrate different ways of navigating the issue of a methods section, including what to expect from a methods section (from the reader's perspective) and how to produce it (from the researcher's perspective).

The first part of the chapter provides an overview of the most common elements that comprise interview reports, such as dissertations, journal articles, or monographs. After this I present three different ways of conceiving of the methods section—as a prelude to the analysis and findings, as a postscript, and as embedded in the interpretation itself—before closing with reflections on how to deal with the idea that, in qualitative interview research, the person of the researcher is the most important "methodological instrument."

Common Elements of an Interview Report

Some years ago, I heard from a colleague[1] that when reading scientific reports, one really needs to pose just two questions to the author (represented by her text):

(1) What do you mean?
(2) How do you know?

Although this may be overly simplistic, there is some truth to it, and while the answer to what the researcher *means* is usually provided in the sections on research findings in the final report, the answer to *how* the researcher knows this (i.e. how she justifies what she means to say) is found in a methods section. How to state clearly what one means and has found out (or how to state it in moving, evocative, enlightening, or original ways) will be treated in the next chapter, on writing up the research findings, while the present chapter addresses how to tell readers *how* one has come to know (what one believes to know).

In standard reports, however, a methods section is just one element, and it only works *as* an element if the researcher has given thought to how it fits into the whole. Thus, I shall here provide an overview of the different elements that commonly go into an interview report. After this, we shall see that many other ways of structuring a report—and not least of thinking about how to communicate methodological issues—are possible.

If you are writing an article, dissertation, or monograph based on qualitative interviewing, and wish to follow the conventions of the trade, you are likely to structure your report into five separate

---

1. Lars Hem from Aarhus University.

chunks (see e.g. Silverman, 2000): An introductory part, a literature review, a methodology part, the findings, and a concluding
part. I shall briefly go through each of these before concentrating
on the methods section in the rest of this chapter.

• *The introduction*: What I mean by an introduction is not
just the first paragraph of text that you are likely to present to the
reader, but also what is sometimes known as the "front matter":
the title, the abstract (compulsory in most journal articles), a list
of contents (if your manuscript is for a book), and the first bit of
prose itself.

The title is the first introduction you provide for the reader, and
it is important to choose a title that is both appealing and informative of the contents. Many qualitative interview papers have
rather long titles that are split in two, separated by a colon. Two of
the articles discussed below illustrate this: Kathy Charmaz (1999)
"Stories of suffering: Subjective tales and research narratives" and
Dana Lee Hansen & Ebba Holme Hansen (2006) "Caught in a
balancing act: Parents' dilemmas regarding their ADHD child's
treatment with stimulant medication." (We have also seen this in
Wacquant, 1995) The words before the colon can point to the overarching theme of the paper (as in Charmaz' case) or the main concept constructed by the researchers (as in the Hansen & Hansen
case), and the colon is usually followed by a somewhat longer and
more precise description of the contents.

It has become widespread practice in interview studies to use
an interviewee statement as the title, and this can be a good idea if
one can find a statement that really pinpoints the main story one
wishes to convey. But sometimes this practice mystifies a little bit
and may lead the reader to expect something that is not actually
realized in the text. On the one hand, the title is like the logo or the
brand name of the text, and should therefore be given serious consideration, but on the other hand, one should not speculate endlessly about how to name the text. It might be useful to formulate
a tentative title when preparing and thematizing the study (see the
previous chapter), and then reformulate the title as one goes along
in the research process, using the title as a constant reminder of
what the focus of the research project should be (which may be
adjusted or changed along the way).

The next thing is the abstract, summarizing the main contents of the text. According to Silverman (2000, p. 222), an abstract should cover the research problem, why this is important to study, what kinds of data are involved and what methods have been used, the main findings, and finally the implications of the study in light of the existing literature. It is almost an art form to summarize all these features in what should often be 150 words or less, but it is actually an exercise that is valuable in itself, and one that researchers may favorably experiment with throughout an interview project (like the title). If one cannot say in 150 words what one means and how one came to know it, then it might be a sign that the research process is not yet completed. That one *can* articulate these matters to colleagues and friends indicates on the other hand that one's analysis is likely to be well-founded and saturated, that one has arrived at some gestalt that can be communicated, and that one is ready to publish or hand in the dissertation.

Concerning the table of contents, the same trick of continually working with this as a research tool in itself can favorably be used. One should not wait until all the research and writing has been done to write a table of contents, but the table should be used productively throughout as a thinking tool. In his book on writing up qualitative research, Wolcott (2009) even goes so far as saying that one should write the table of contents when drafting a research/dissertation *proposal* (p. 14). Again, the table of contents can work as an organizing tool in the research process. When the researcher is forced to keep the end product continually in view, the result will ideally be that the (sometimes overwhelming) whole of the text is broken down into manageable units that one can address one by one.

Wolcott also has useful advice for how to begin the actual text of the research report. His advice is that your first sentence is a variant of "The purpose of this study is…" (Wolcott, 2009, p. 14). I used this semantic construction myself in opening this book in the preface. It might seem to be quite boring as a beginning, but it has two great advantages: First, it enables the researcher/writer to keep in focus what the purpose is throughout the process of writing. As an editor of journals and books, I can say that *the* main problem of qualitative writings is (a lack of) focus—not concentrating on the story that one is telling, not having a clear message, etc. And second, again speaking as editor and reader of interview studies, beginning a text with a clear statement of purpose has the great advantage of reminding readers of what they are actually reading. It is so easy for the reader to go back to the first line and be reminded of the purpose of the study. It is common for writers of interview reports to forget that their readers are not as knowledgeable of the research project as the researchers themselves, and what may seem trivial to the writers (who might have worked on this subject for years) can be original and difficult to grasp for the reader, who might be reading about interviews with people with Alzheimer's disease (or something else) for the first time. One should never underestimate the reader, of course, but a clear and visible statement of the purpose of the study is a simple and effective pedagogical tool that has nothing to do with underestimation.

A good purpose statement often does more than simply point to the theme of the paper/dissertation/book. It also informs the reader of *how* the researcher will approach the theme. Using Hammersley's concepts, which I discussed in the previous chapter, it is often helpful if the researcher tells the reader whether the study was set up to *discover* unknown features of the given theme, to *construct* a new social practice, or to *understand* something better about social life. So the choice of the verb in the first sentence is very important: "The purpose of this study is to discover/construct/understand..." (and the list of possible relevant verbs could be made much longer: describe, explain, interpret, analyze, deconstruct, criticize, give voice to, etc.).

After being told the purpose of the study, the reader would normally like to know why the researcher has chosen this particular topic, why it is interesting, and what methodological approach the researcher has adopted. For interview reports, unsurprisingly, it should be stated that the study is an interview project, and it is also common to articulate one's main theoretical standpoint (e.g. phenomenology or discourse analysis). I also personally appreciate it when the researcher informs readers of her conception of interviewing (cf. the first chapter of this book).

• *The literature review*: In qualitative research (as in other forms of research), we nearly always stand on the shoulders of previous researchers, and what is conventionally known as the literature review is meant to situate a given contribution in a body of work that has already been done. Even if one does not wish to stand on the shoulders of someone else, but, for example, intends to climb down from them (!) and go somewhere else, it is still relevant to tell the readers that these "shoulders" exist, so that one can provide some kind of critical distance to them, if that is one's goal as a researcher. The literature review should give the reader a clear idea of why the research was worth doing in light of what has already been done in the field. So, in order to be able to assess the worthiness of the research project, (and to be able to decide whether to spend time reading the rest of the text), the reader, should be informed about research that has already been done on the theme of interest.

It is difficult to present clear guidelines for the scope and length of the literature review. It may range from a few lines that mention all existing studies about a well-defined problem (e.g. qualitative studies of parents' attitudes to ADHD medicine) and how the present study contributes to the discussion, to entire meta-syntheses of qualitative studies. Meta-synthesis, which analyzes already published studies in order to arrive at new meta-interpretations of a specific theme, is a genre of qualitative research in its own right and exceeds normal literature reviews (see Noblit & Hare, 1988, for an early introduction to the art of synthesizing qualitative studies into meta-syntheses). But the logic of providing an overview of research in an area, and evaluating previous studies in light of current concerns, is similar in literature reviews and meta-syntheses. The virtue of a proper meta-synthesis is normally its thoroughness, which results in a long text that can easily form an entire paper in itself, whereas in most journal articles, a literature review is much shorter. And, as Wolcott reminds us, readers generally want to be engaged immediately with the problem addressed, rather than having to read pages and pages of how learned the researcher has become (Wolcott, 2009, p. 68).

It is common to begin a research project by writing a literature review (e.g. in order to identify gaps in the literature that one's research may attempt to fill). This is standard practice in most doctoral research projects, but Silverman interestingly suggests the opposite: "Write notes on your reading but don't attempt to write your literature review chapter early on in your research." (Silverman, 2000, p. 230). His main reason for this is that a literature review is in principle a never-ending process. There always seems to be "just one more" book or article to read in the topical area, and researchers run the risk of beginning the actual interviews and analyses too late by spending too much time on the literature review. I agree that this is a constant danger, but I also believe in the usefulness of doing a literature review early on in the research process, as this will likely be a source of inspiration for what to do—and what *not* to do—in one's own project. Doing the literature review is not necessarily boring, and it may even be very inspirational when one learns about the successes (and failures) of others. Having a firm deadline for when to begin (and end) the data collection phase might help you get out of the library in time.

• *The methods section*: After telling the reader about other studies in the area, the methods section is normally the next chunk of text in an interview report. Below, I shall present three ways of thinking about the methods section (as prelude, as postscript, and as embedded or integrated in the text itself). So instead of repeating here what a methods section should encompass, and where it should be placed in the overall text, I shall briefly refer to Silverman, who has pointed to several aspects of qualitative research that researchers need to recognize when writing up the methods section: (1) The contested theoretical underpinnings of qualitative methodologies, (2) the often contingent nature of qualitative data, and (3) the likely nonrandom character of the cases (Silverman, 2000, p. 234).

Qualitative interviewers should not feel guilty or less important (in comparison with quantitative peers) when pondering these aspects, but all of these issues should be confronted directly and constructively. Concerning the first one, as this book also testifies, a large number of theoretical schools exist within qualitative research, some of which are coupled to epistemologies and philosophies while others are coupled more directly to specific methodological procedures. If it has not already been made clear earlier in a research report, the theoretical assumptions behind the methodology should be spelled out in the methods section. Is the study phenomenological, involving a specific style of interviewing and analysis of interviewing, or is it social constructionist, seeking to use the conversations as transformational engines in some local social practice?

Next, concerning the second aspect, there is nothing intrinsically wrong about the fact that the data of qualitative studies often rest on contingent factors (e.g. if one has not really selected participants according to some representative logic, but had to make do with whomever happened to be available). It is only wrong if one is not clear about the process of recruiting participants, for example. The contingent factors should be spelled out, and the implications of the contingencies for the research project should be reflected upon (which one may return to later in the text when discussing possible limitations of the study).

Finally, about the third aspect, qualitative analyses may be useful and enlightening even when based on very small bodies of nonrandom data, and they might still be used as a basis for some kind of generalization of the results. If the issue of generalization is important for the researcher's project, the researcher should provide an argument telling the reader how a small study may have wider implications (see e.g. the discussion of deduction in the previous chapter). In qualitative inquiry, it is rarely the number of participants in itself that is important for generalization, but the craftsmanship of the analysis. The goal of interview studies is not to impress the reader with *how much* you have done (e.g. a huge number of interviews), but with *how well* you have conducted and analyzed the interviews (Wolcott, 2009, p. 40).

Although qualitative researchers should recognize the unique features of their methods, they should not make excuses but should explain why it can be important to interview, say, seven people who have been sent to prison on illegitimate grounds. Fortunately, the times have changed in most disciplines, so that there is today much less need for defending qualitative inquiry than before. The best strategy might be not to defend it explicitly at all, but to present instead a well-crafted, thought-provoking analysis that shows readers that interview studies can be of high quality. Showing rather than telling is often of great significance in qualitative work. The tree of qualitative interviewing shall be known by its fruits, and not just by sophisticated philosophical arguments about the legitimacy of this method.

I will return to the contents of the methods section below, but the questions to be answered by a methods section are nicely summarized by Silverman (2000, p. 235):

- How did you go about your research?
- What overall strategy did you use and why?
- What design and techniques did you employ?
- Why these and not others?

The key word here is *why*. The reader needs more than *descriptions* of the methodological procedures, however informative these may be of the procedure of recruitment, number of participants, analytic practices etc. In addition, a *justification* is needed that tells the reader *why* this particular way of studying the world can lead to new discoveries, constructions, or understandings (cf. the previous chapter) of the conversational worlds of human beings. The reader usually approaches a text with an implicit why-question in her mind anyway, and it is definitely preferable if the researcher raises this question herself and explains it in her own words to the reader. For example: "Let me tell you why interviewing five people about their experiences of X, and analyzing their descriptions by doing Y, can lead to interesting answers to my research question Z."

- *The findings section*: The next chapter of the present book is devoted in its entirety to descriptions and discussions of how to write up the research findings, so here I shall simply include a few words about how to think of the findings in relation to the research text as a whole. In most papers and books, the parts devoted to the findings are normally the longest ones. This is as it should be, since researchers who have actually discovered, constructed, or understood something that they did not know before their interviews and analyses will naturally allocate most of the pages to telling the reader about this, rather than talking about how they came to know what they arguably know. To use an analogy: If one has found gold, it is understandable that one spends a lot of time describing the gold (the findings) instead of rambling on about the spade (the method) that one has employed in digging.

The analogy is clear, but it is also potentially misleading. For, in gold digging, one actually finds something that is *there*, to be unearthed, and which more or less comes in the same way and amount regardless of one's way of digging. As we saw in the first chapter of this book, this is not so in qualitative interviewing. Here, the data are not so much unearthed (i.e. found) as they are produced in the situated interaction of the interviewer and interviewee. Some constructionists will even argue that data are *constructed*; that they are in that sense a unique function of the relationship between the two conversationalists. Even if you believe that this conclusion implies taking one step too far, and adhere to the common-sense view that people can use conversations to say something interesting about extra-conversational features of the world, it is still problematic to treat the findings (the gold) in abstraction from the methods (the spade). In qualitative interviewing, there are close relationships between data, theory, and methodology in relation to the findings, as illustrated in the triangle below.

Figure 3.1 is meant to illustrate the idea that findings, in qualitative research, are never just a product of data, nor of "data analysis" in itself. One of the key criticisms of the logical positivists in the first half of the 20th century was that they treated data as simply given, as amenable to being inductively put together and then being informative of something. But this naïve inductive approach overlooked the fact that data are always codetermined by theory and methodology. Working with data without theory and methodology makes you blind—just as pure theoretical speculations easily become empty. Only by putting data, theory, and methodology together will findings emerge in an analytic process. As we have seen, these three are often treated separately in a research report, but really good findings sections usually find a way of integrating them to show in writing how the findings came to be in a mutual relationship with all legs of the triangle. Doing this elegantly and convincingly is difficult, and we return to the issue in the next chapter. The point here has simply been to stress (once again) that no aspect of the research

Figure 3.1. The Data-Theory-Methodology Triangle

process—just as no element in the written text—can be thought of in abstraction from the whole. A good interview report mirrors the dynamism of the interviews themselves.

The findings section is usually followed by a discussion, which might also be integrated into the findings section itself. A good discussion can return to methodological issues and evaluate the role of the concrete practice of interviewing in relation to the findings, or it may connect and compare the findings to the extant literature, thus returning to the literature review. It is always important to construct an argument in the text that moves forward in some way, builds on or returns to other elements of the text, not necessarily in a linear and cumulative manner, but sometimes in a manner that brings out complexities, different and contradictory layers of social life, and also highlights multiple possible readings and interpretations of the given materials.

- *The conclusion*: There are mixed opinions about how to conclude the text of an interview study. On one side, we have editors of the journals that are fond of standardized formats, which involve ending the paper with some kind of summary, perhaps followed by implications or recommendations for practice, or reflections on the kind of research that is needed in the field in the future. More research always seems to be needed, and (on a personal note) it could be refreshing to read a study, just once, which concluded that enough research has now been done on a specific theme or phenomenon! (I honestly believe that this conclusion should sometimes be drawn, although I have never seen it in practice). On the other side, we have people who are more conscious of style such as Wolcott, whose answer to the question "How do you conclude a qualitative study?" is "You don't." (Wolcott, 2009, p. 113). He continues advising his reader: "Give serious thought to dropping the idea that your final chapter must lead to a conclusion or that the account must build toward a dramatic climax." (p. 113).

I agree with Wolcott (who also advises against using the word "findings," as this term signals something too conclusive) that in a philosophical sense, there are no conclusions in qualitative work; the basic issues under scrutiny will always remain open to further interpretations and new re-descriptions and stories. As I argued in Chapter 1, the conversational world that we study in qualitative interviewing is a never-ending process. But I also think that Wolcott makes too much of the word "conclusion," and that the conclusion section, like the abstract and table of contents, can be a great pedagogical aid to readers as well as the researcher herself. Unlike the abstract and table of contents, however, I do believe that the conclusion should be the last thing that you write, and that you should take care to provide a nice ending to your account that displays fidelity to the work that you have done along with the research participants, and which not merely says the exact same thing as the body of the text, but points further and directs the reader's attention to possible implications of your argument.

The Methods Section as Prelude

After going through the main elements of common interview reports, I will demonstrate three ways of thinking about the methods section specifically. The first model is as a *prelude* to the analysis, findings, and interpretations, and—as always in qualitative inquiry—the best way to inform is by showing rather than telling. So, I shall show how the methods section can be included as a prelude by way of an example. It is more or less chosen by random, although it is an interview study that concerns a theme that I am greatly interested in, viz. the diagnosis ADHD (attention deficit/hyperactive disorder) and the current medical treatment used against the symptoms. In Box 3.1, I quote large parts of the methods section from a study of parents' dilemmas regarding treating their children (diagnosed with ADHD) with stimulant medication (Hansen & Hansen, 2006).

Box 3.1 **The Methods Section as Prelude: An Example**

Before the methods section cited below, the authors of the exemplary paper have (1) begun their paper with an introduction that sets the scene by providing some statistics about the prevalence of ADHD and also a couple of paragraphs that sum up the previous studies of parents' decisions and beliefs about treating their children with ADHD medicine. Since there were just a few studies about this, the literature review could be included in the introduction in this way. The authors then (2) very briefly described the theoretical perspective of the study, which is grounded in the phenomenology of Husserl and Schutz. Then follows the methods section as a prelude to the findings:

"As is typical for studies conducted from the constructivist standpoint, we aimed at gaining a deeper understanding of parents' lifeworlds [...]. Thus, we made no attempt to design a study from which the results of a representative sample could be generalized to a larger population. A suitable method for carrying out user perspective studies is the qualitative interview [...], which has the potential to provide a detailed and personal insight into subjects' lifeworlds [...]. Consequently, data were collected via in-depth semistructured interviews with the parents.

Recruitment of parents was based on a convenience sampling in two cities located in the Canadian province of Alberta. Prior to recruitment of participants, the study was approved by the Community Research Ethics Board of Alberta (Protocol No. 0403). Recruitment for the study took place via two routes. One was through local child psychiatrists, who contacted parents by phone or mentioned the study during a consultation. Contact to the majority of the participating parents was arranged through an ADHD advocacy group.

The study's focus on parents' everyday experiences with stimulant treatment for ADHD determined the inclusion criteria for participation. Thus, parents who had experienced having their ADHD-diagnosed son or daughter receive treatment with stimulant medication for at least a 6-month period were included in the study.

Ten parents were recruited for the study. Most of the children with ADHD were boys ($n = 9$). Only 2 were girls. Children ranged in age from 8 to 22. Approximately half ($n = 6$) of the children had comorbidities. Nine of the children were taking stimulant medication at the time of the interview, whereas the other 2 had terminated the treatment. The total number of children in the family varied from 1 to 4. Between them, the informants had 11 children with the diagnosis ADHD. Only 1 father participated in the study. The other 9 parents were mothers. Parents' ages ranged from 29 to 56 years. The majority of the participants were married, but 2 were divorced. Parents had a wide range of occupations, and some of the mothers were full time homemakers. Epidemiological data show that the group studied was, in two respects, typical of parents of ADHD children in general. In the sample families, the greater number of boys with ADHD, as well as the presence of comorbidities, corresponds to the reported difference in prevalence between the sexes and in regards to the prevalence of comorbid disorders [...].

Interviews were conducted by DLH [the first author] in the spring of 2004. Each interview was audiotaped for later transcription. The duration of the interviews was approximately 1½ to 2 hours. All informants chose to have the interview take place in their own home. Informed consent was obtained in written form from each parent before the interview was started. At this time, parents also completed a short questionnaire eliciting basic demographic information and background information regarding the children's diagnosis and treatment.

Several sources of information and inspiration were used in the development of the interview guide. Existing literature on the subject was drawn on, as well as interview transcripts from a documentary film about ADHD [...] and an Internet chat forum for parents of children with ADHD (ADHD News). In addition, a 2-week observational period at a child psychiatrist practice in Edmonton, Alberta, served to inform the interview guide as well as sensitize the interviewer to the later interviews.

The interview guide addressed several themes related specifically to the medication therapy: decisions about treatment, perceptions of and experiences with the medication, and the medication's role or meaning in the family's everyday life. Throughout the interview, open-ended questions encouraging reflexive, descriptive, and lengthy answers were posed.

During the stages of interview transcription and analysis, clear procedural guidelines were set up and followed for each interview. The interviews provided a sound basis for interpretation, as the quality of the recordings was good, making it possible to transcribe each interview verbatim. In keeping with a phenomenological approach, the method of reduction was used to analyze the interview data [...]. Significant statements were selected and transferred to condensation tables and later categorized according to themes developing in the data. Furthermore, interpretation was inspired by Pollio, Henley, and Thompson's (1997) existential phenomenology, as the inductive procedure employed was based on a part-to-whole analysis. The part-to-whole analysis was carried out on three levels, as comparisons were continually made within thematic categories and within the context of the original interview, as well as within the context of the entire interview set as a whole.

The 10 interviews conducted were sufficient in providing a rich insight into parents' everyday experiences with ADHD and its treatment. One by one, the first 5 interviews resulted in a wealth of new themes. These themes were enriched and developed through the following interviews, and thematic saturation was reached around the eighth interview, as new themes did not appear after this point. This approach is supported by Kvale (1996), who noted that the number of interviews in current studies is generally around 15 ± 10.

During the process of interview analysis, many safeguards were taken to ensure that the results reflected the parents' perspective. Following the phenomenological tradition, epoché was sought though bracketing of personal knowledge and experience [...]. In addition, the transcribed interviews were considered to be interpretive constructions (Kvale, 1996). Thus, transcription conventions that made the interview stay as "alive" as possible and best conveyed the original interview situation were chosen. Rather than forcing the data into predetermined categories arising from the interview guide, we allowed thematic categories to develop out of the data. Furthermore, parents' own terms were used in the written interpretations and meaning condensations. Interpretation was carried out at the level of the informant's self understanding, and no attempt was made to find abstract meanings in parents' statements. Validity was further secured by having both researchers participate in the formation of the interview guide and later analysis and interpretation of the transcribed interviews, thus guarding against the interviewer imposing her own personal interpretations." (adapted from Hansen & Hansen, 2006, pp. 1270–1272; I have omitted some references, marked by [...]).

The paper on parents' dilemmas regarding treating their children diagnosed with ADHD medically is a good example of how to use the methods section as a prelude to a presentation of the findings, and it succeeds in compressing a huge amount of information into a few paragraphs. Obviously, one could always demand more description of methodological procedures, but, in this case, as a reader, I do not miss any pieces of information. The paper thus illustrates how one can succinctly summarize answers to the following methodological questions in a methods section:

- Why interviews and not some other method? As I have touched upon earlier in this book, this question is too often omitted, when researchers take for granted that interviews represent the proper way of answering a specific research question. In the Hansen and Hansen example, the researchers actually do provide a reason why qualitative interviewing is needed and adequate in their case.
- How were the participants recruited? This involves describing sampling and selection, which, in this case, is referred to as convenience sampling by the authors.
- Has the study been approved of by an ethics committee? There are huge regional differences concerning requirements for ethical approval, but, at least when writing for an international audience, it is usually relevant to inform the reader about any formal ethical procedures.
- How many participants were included? In this case, ten parents of children diagnosed with ADHD.
- What are the characteristics of the participants? Children or adults? Men or women? Countless characteristics can be included, but information should be limited to those characteristics that are relevant in relation to the research theme. In this case, the child's sex and age, and the also the parent's sex were deemed important.
- When were the interviews conducted and by whom? It is not unusual to publish papers based on interviews that were conducted many years ago, so information about when they were conducted can be important. Also, it is not necessarily the researcher or the first author herself that has acted as interviewer (although in this case it was), so it is also relevant to include this kind of information.

- How long were the interviews and where were they conducted? In this case, the interviews took place in the participants' homes.
- Were the interviews recorded and transcribed? Not all interviews are recorded, so information about this should be stated, preferably along with information about the procedure of transcribing the interviews.
- How did the researcher obtain informed consent? This may be particularly challenging in qualitative research, where the focus of the research project may change in the investigative process, giving rise to a need for ongoing negotiation of consent (this, however, was not relevant in the example).
- How was the interview guide constructed? In the example, the authors describe the sources of inspiration for the guide and also which themes that ended up being included.
- Which method of analysis was employed? In this case, the authors subscribe to phenomenology and provide a very brief description of their analytic procedures.
- Why are the chosen number of interviewees sufficient? The authors explain that they reached a certain thematic saturation in their analysis after analyzing around 8 interviews, which signals that no additional themes are likely to emerge by doing further interviews. Many interview reports skip this point and wrongly presuppose that readers can implicitly acknowledge why the given number of participants was logical or sufficient.
- What is the main analytic aim? In this case, it was understanding the parents' life world at a level of self-understanding, which means that a valid analysis is said to be one that the participants can recognize. This, of course, is not necessarily so, as other, more theoretical, readings of the materials would also have been possible.
- Who performed the analyses? Again, since research today is often carried out by large teams, it is not given that the first author is the sole analyst, and, in this case, we learn that both authors of the paper were involved in constructing the interview guide as well as in analyzing and interpreting the statements.

If you want to publish in a journal that might not be open to non-traditional qualitative formats, or if you study in a department that is unfamiliar with qualitative methodologies, it is probably a good idea to have the methods section of your interview report early in the text—as a prelude to the findings—and to take a rather standardized approach. If your methods section includes answers to all of the questions that are raised above, your text will likely satisfy most readers in terms of methodological description. In that way, these questions can favorably be used as a checklist when writing the methods section.

The Methods Section as Postscript

Instead of having the methods section before the findings and results, you might want to tell readers as early as possible in your text about the exciting things you have discovered or understood through your interviews. If so, you can include the methods section as a postscript. If this is done well, the reader will initially be drawn into the interesting stories, descriptions, and analyses that ensued from the interviews, and may subsequently wonder: "Well, that was great! But how did the researcher arrive at these results—how did this knowledge come about?" And the methods section will, as a postscript, provide answers to these questions. Again, an example may serve to illustrate how this can be done.

Box 3.2 **The methods section as postscript: An example**

....

Kathy Charmaz, who is well known in qualitative research circles because of her constructivist interpretations of grounded theory (e.g. Charmaz, 2011), has also published on people's experiences of chronic illness. In a moving paper based on interviews with patients, nested within an ethnographic approach to qualitative inquiry, she begins *in medias res* by telling the story of a woman with different and difficult medical problems, whom Charmaz has been interviewing for seven years. One is immediately drawn into the text, lured by the evocative, yet precise, prose crafted by the author. We then hear stories from other participants as well, and Charmaz provides readers with a typology of possible forms of suffering, and she also presents the theoretical foundations of her work (symbolic interactionism).

The crux of the analysis is an understanding of the moral status involved in suffering, and Charmaz constructs a model—a hierarchy of moral status in suffering—based on her interviews with patients. As such, I believe the paper is a solid, interesting, and evocative piece of work that shows what suffering is (and does not just "tell" it). The descriptions and analyses are followed by a "methodological epilogue" (which comes *after* the conclusion) that begins with two significant questions: "How do we tell an analytic story about our respondents' stories? Which research and writing methods can we use to portray their stories?" (Charmaz, 1999, p. 375). And Charmaz answers:

"Our subjects tell a tale and piece together puzzles from their past. They may need to re-view and restitch events to weave a seamless tale. What sounds seamless and complete to them may not to us. The meaning of the tale may be invisible, incomplete, or even incomprehensible. Then we have to piece their tales together to discover what they mean from our vantage point. Finding analytic meaning requires that we listen for cues, look for clues, and then pursue them. It entails being willing to go back to people—sometimes again and again. The further we delve into implicit meanings, the more we may need to wonder and watch.

The predominant method of studying the experience of illness consists of conducting one-shot interviews. An initial interview may not elicit complete information, much less implicit meanings. Researchers cannot expect to get beneath the surface with every respondent in one visit. We need to build trust and to create a safe place in which they can disclose thoughts and feelings as well as facts and acts. Researcher and respondent more or less co-construct interviews from which a respondent's story emerges. This story is neither absolute truth nor fiction. Through our interviews, however, we should aim to gain an inner view of our respondents and how they see their worlds [...].

Conceptions of moral claims and moral status in suffering did not jump out of the data into my ready hands. If the ideas were right there, they eluded me. However, much material that indicated such concerns did reside on the surface of the interviews. Many respondents divulged tales of feeling stigmatized, of being judged negatively, and of feeling different and separate. A few hinted at their moral superiority vis-à-vis their diagnostic peers. They made invidious comparisons between how they and others handled their conditions. I sensed their claims to superiority, but I did not connect them to the moral status of suffering. Only through hearing multiple voices and comparing many tales did these ideas take form. To see these moral issues involved going into a liminal place deep within the experience rather than surveying its surface.

My analysis of suffering developed from a grounded theory study of the body and self. In keeping with the grounded theory method, I wrote memos about my emerging ideas during the data collection [...]. These early memos focused on the body in illness, not on suffering per se, but they moved me toward developing ideas (and memos) about suffering later. Memo writing is the pivotal intermediate step between coding data and writing the first draft of the analysis. Memo writing helps researchers to define and delineate theoretical categories and to focus further data collection. This analytic step is crucial because it keeps researchers in control of their studies. The following list describes the advantages of memo writing [...].

Memo writing helps researchers to

- stop and think about data;
- develop a writer's voice and writing rhythm (Memos can read like letters to a close friend; there is no need for stodgy academic prose.);
- spark ideas to check out in the field setting;
- avoid forcing data into extant theories;
- treat qualitative codes as categories to analyze;
- clarify categories—define them, state their properties, and delineate their conditions, consequences, connections with other categories;
- make explicit comparisons—data with data, category with category, and concept with concept;
- develop fresh ideas, create concepts, and find novel relationships;
- demonstrate connections between categories (e.g., empirical events and social structures, larger groups and the individual, espoused beliefs and actions);

- discover gaps in data collection;
- link data gathering with data analysis and report writing;
- build whole sections of papers and chapters;
- keep involved in research and writing; and
- increase confidence and competence.

The lines between the analytic and writing phases of research blur. Discovery processes and conceptual development proceed into the writing. Researchers may act as if their writing is mere reporting. However, writing is a way of learning and of gaining precision and clarity. Qualitative researchers can find that their arguments and emphases arise in their written drafts rather than in earlier memos and conceptual maps.

Like essayists and storytellers, scientific writers use rhetorical devices, metaphors, and writing strategies to explain their findings to their audiences. We can also adapt writing strategies from fiction writers to improve our craft as long as we remain faithful to our studied experience in the field." (adapted from Charmaz, 1999, pp. 375–377; I have omitted some references, marked by [...]).

After this methodological epilogue, Charmaz provides some helpful guidelines for ethnographic writing, but I shall not summarize them here, since writing up the research findings will be a topic for the next chapter.

We see that Charmaz' methodological description in Box 3.2 is very different from the previous one in Box 3.1. It is much harder to spell out Charmaz' approach in bullet points or check lists, since what she offers us is a description of coming to *understand* something, viz. the stories people tell of suffering. She writes in the first person about how she has engaged with the data, and how, in the analytic process leading up to the final article, the lines between the phases of analysis and writing have blurred. When doing interpretative work in this way, writing is analyzing is writing is analyzing... Or, as Richardson and St. Pierre have put it: Writing is a method of inquiry in itself (Richardson & St.Pierre, 2005).

Charmaz does make explicit, however, that she has worked from a grounded theory perspective, where memo writing is a crucial technique, and her list of the different functions of memos ought to be helpful for all qualitative researchers (even for those who do not follow grounded theory guidelines), since memo writing in some form or another is an element in almost all forms of analysis. All in all, the methods section by Charmaz, included in her paper as a postscript (or epilogue, as she says), can be called a sketch of a phenomenology of how to work methodologically with interviews. It does not make discrete methodical steps explicit, but it seeks to describe, from her own perspective, what she has actually done. In that way, her paper is not only a fine analysis of a significant phenomenon in human lives, but also a piece that educates the reader in analyzing and writing stories of suffering.

Another example of the methods section as postscript is found in the study by Bellah and colleagues (1985) that I have referred to earlier. They present the methodological considerations as an appendix, which, however, is an extremely interesting discussion about how to use interviews actively in generating a Socratic dialogue about moral issues. But again, readers are primarily convinced by the findings and analyses that comprise the book as such and not by the methodological appendix.

The Embedded Methods Section

In addition to (1) including the methods section early on in an interview report, and clearly articulating the methodological steps that have been taken in a research project, and (2) having the methods section as a postscript, describing the process of coming to understand from a first-person perspective, it is also possible (3) to avoid having a separate methods section altogether and, instead, to write up the methodological details in a way that embeds and integrates them into the text as a whole.

We have already seen an example of this. In Box 2.3 in the previous chapter, we saw an example of how to engage in qualitative interviewing with the aim of understanding a social practice (boxing) through immersing oneself in it (Wacquant, 1995). In the process, the researcher became an insider and was able to conduct interviews with participants in the practice. These interviews would have been impossible had the interviewer not done this specific kind of participant observation for years and acquired "the pugilistic point of view." In Wacquant's text, there is actually a short paragraph with a description of the methodology (on p. 493), but this is merely a small drop of methods in what is a large (and pleasant) sea of almost fifty journal pages. The main methodological descriptions are embedded in the analytic text as whole—built in, one could say, in the narratives themselves, when Wacquant reports them. Thus, when we are introduced to a boxer with whom Wacquant has talked, we typically read a little bit about this person's background and his relationship with the researcher. The reader is provided with the information necessary to understand what has happened and what is said in the interview, just when it is needed. This kind of embedded methods section, distributed throughout the paper, results in a very readable text, which gives the reader a sense of being close to the persons interviewed. As a reader, one can follow the flow of the research process instead of having the process broken up into separate elements.

Another study, which now stands as a classic example of how to do and report interview research creatively, is the book *Troubling the Angels—Women living with HIV/AIDS* by Patti Lather and Chris Smithies (1997) (see also the discussion in Kvale & Brinkmann, 2008, p. 288). In the course of doing the research, the researchers talked with HIV-positive women, both in their support groups and individually, and depicted their struggles and sufferings from the time of being infected to being diagnosed and through to dying. The book is organized experimentally as different layers of various kinds of information that are represented visually on the book pages. The main parts report conversations from support groups for the women, with the researchers entering with questions and comments at times.

The style of writing mirrors the chaotic and polyphonic nature of postmodern life. The stories of the women are interspersed with intermezzos on angels that chronicle the social and cultural issues raised by the disease. Factual information on HIV/AIDS is presented in boxes throughout the text, and across the bottom of large parts of the book is a running commentary by the researchers that moves between descriptions and discussions of research methods and theoretical frameworks to include aspects of the researchers' own lives, with their reactions to the research theme. The interview book by Lather and Smithies has, in this way, a methods section that is distributed across the interview text, enabling the reader to continuously follow the analytic thoughts of the researchers as they are engaged with their participants. With this style of writing up the methodology, there is no longer a relevant distinction between methods, findings, theory, and data, for they all come together in the writing.

The Person Is the Instrument: A Note of Caution about Methodology

When the methodological ideas and reflections of an interview report are embedded and distributed across the text as a whole, the result may be likened to the goods manufactured by craftspersons. In the crafts, it is the product itself that is evaluated and not specific methods. One may use food as an analogy: While mass-produced foods come with a long list of ingredients attached (and how these were "methodologically" put together), top cuisine speaks for itself, in a way. One trusts the chef and evaluates the product with no need for specific information about the making of the food. The quality of the product is not linked to specific methods, but to the excellence of the end result as such.

Conceiving of qualitative research as a craft, rather than something based on methodological rules that can be made explicit, is inspired by the writings of the sociologist C. Wright Mills (1959), who argued that as a craft, much of the knowledge of social researchers is tacit and tied to the person rather than to method (What follows builds on Brinkmann, 2012b.) In the 1950s, Mills depicted social research in general as "intellectual craftsmanship," and, in this light, although mastery of the relevant methods are important for the craft of social research, the methods should not become autonomous idols of scientific inquiry. Methods, Mills argued, "are like the language of the country you live in; it is nothing to brag about that you can speak it, but it is a disgrace and an inconvenience if you cannot" (Mills, 1959, p. 121). Instead of using methods mechanically and subsequently reporting them as such (in a "methods section"), Mills believed in the power of the researcher-craftsperson herself to generate insightful research. Here is a famous quote from Mills:

> Be a good craftsman: Avoid any rigid set of procedures. Above all, seek to develop and to use the sociological imagination. Avoid the fetishism of method and technique. Urge the rehabilitation of the unpretentious intellectual craftsman, and try to become such a craftsman yourself. Let every man be his own methodologist; let every man be his own theorist; let theory and method again become part of the practice of a craft (Mills, 1959, p. 224).

Recently, anthropologist Tim Ingold (2011) has rehabilitated Mills' plea for intellectual craftsmanship, destroying traditional divisions between "theory" and "method." We do not (or should not) begin social research with a theoretical agenda that is then operationalized into testable hypotheses through methods, Ingold argues. Rather, we should acknowledge, as he says, "that there is no division, in practice, between work and life. [An intellectual craft] is a practice that involves the whole person, continually drawing on past experience as it is projected into the future." (p. 240). We should never forget that we do qualitative research for purposes of living, and methods are simply some of the tools we employ in the process, and, as tools, they are in a way much less interesting than what we may construct when using the tools.

The crafts approach to qualitative research is one that tries to avoid the dangers of "methodolatry" (idolizing methods) on the one hand, and a mysterious reliance on subjective intuition on the other. To mechanically follow certain prespecified methodological steps does not guarantee scientific truth, let alone interesting research. Rather than distrusting our ordinary human capacities for observing and communicating about our lives, and allocating understanding to specific methods instead, we might focus on the person of the researcher as the actual research instrument itself. This was expressed, for example, by anthropologist Jean Lave in the following interview sequence, where Steinar Kvale (SK) acts as interviewer:

SK: Is there an anthropological method? If yes, what is an anthro-pological method?

JL: I think it is complete nonsense to say that we have a method. First of all I don't think that anyone should have *a* method. But in the sense that there are "instruments" that characterise the "methods" of different disciplines—sociological surveys, ques-tionnaire methods, in psychology various kinds of tests and also experiments—there are some very specific technical ways of inquiring into the world. Anthropologists refuse to take those as proper ways to study human being[s]. I think the most gen-eral view is that the only instrument that is sufficiently complex to comprehend and learn about human existence is another human. And so what you use is your own life and your own experience in the world (Lave & Kvale, 1995, p. 220).

As an anecdote, I would like to add that after having written an international bestseller on the method of interviewing, and having read countless doctoral dissertations based on interviewing as well as numerous research proposals, Steinar Kvale (my supervisor and mentor) came to the conclusion—toward the end of his life—that there is a negative correlation between the number of pages devoted to methodology and the quality of a manuscript that communicates qualitative research. The more methodology, the less valuable the contribution, was his general analysis. "Why so," I once asked him, when he revealed this surprisingly negative attitude toward methodology. "Because," he answered, "those who have discovered something novel and important through their studies will focus on *what* is new and exciting, whereas those who have not really found anything of interest can always fill their manuscript with sections on methodology." (I touched upon this earlier when I used the analogy of gold and the spade.) He added that it might not be a coincidence that significant analysts of our time, such as Richard Sennett or Robert Bellah, whose work has been addressed previously in this book, who do in fact use qualitative interviews quite extensively, do *not* in general have lengthy method sections in their books and papers.

These remarks should not be taken to mean that articles without methods sections (or with embedded methodological descriptions) are necessarily better than those with more traditional methods sections. Even if Steinar Kvale was right about the correlation, we should remember that correlation is not causality. There certainly exist excellent interview reports with standard methods sections (and bad interview reports without them), and with or without a separate methods section, the researcher should always strive to make clear how she has come to know what she reports. Not just "what do you mean," but also "how do you know" remains an important question.

When the person is the research instrument, one common path to making how-do-you-know clear involves describing and analyzing the research instrument itself, which is often conceived as researcher *reflexivity*. Kvale and Brinkmann (2008, p. 242) interpret this as a demand for objectivity in the sense of *reflexive objectivity*. This implies being reflexive about one's contributions as a researcher to the production of knowledge. While objectivity is sometimes denied to qualitative inquiry (by insiders as well as outsiders to the craft of qualitative research), it might be important to reinterpret objectivity in terms that suit the specifics of qualitative interviewing.

Striving for objectivity about subjectivity can take a *confessional* form (telling the story of how episodes in one's own life led one to *this* research theme in *this* particular way) or a more *analytical* form (which can include thoughts on the role of the position as researcher in generating talk in an interview). I believe that the latter form is always important, and I have argued at length in Chapter 1 that it is important to reflect on the role of qualitative interviewing as a knowledge-producing social practice. In the language of hermeneutics, we can only make informed judgments, e.g. in research reports, on the basis of our prejudices (literally pre-judgments) that enable us to understand something (Gadamer, 1960). Some of these prejudices are personal (and can be "confessed"), but most of them, I believe, relate to the social practices of knowledge production, such as interviewing. The researcher should attempt to gain insight into these unavoidable prejudices and write about them whenever it seems called for in relation to the research project. Striving for sensitivity about one's prejudices, e.g. one's subjectivity as interviewer and qualitative analyst, involves a reflexive objectivity, i.e. reflexivity about the research instrument.

Conclusion

In this chapter, I first presented the elements that are commonly put together to comprise an interview report, whether they take the forms of a journal article, a dissertation, or a book manuscript. There can be very good reasons to divert from the standard practice when putting together a research report, but there can be equally good reasons for keeping to the standards of the practice. If one wishes to inform a certain research field or discipline about important new findings (e.g. in qualitative health research), it might be important simply to follow standard practice and focus on the results. In other cases, one might be incapable of communicating the findings without a nontraditional writing format, since the *how* of writing can influence *what* one can say.

So, as always in qualitative research, there is no "gold standard," but everything depends on the nature and purpose of the study. I presented three broad ways of thinking about the methods section: a conventional way that inserts the methodological ideas before the analyses and findings, a less traditional way that reports the methodological issues in a postscript, and finally a more experimental way that integrates methodology into the research narrative itself, so that it becomes difficult or impossible to say what the methodology is and what the findings are in separation from each other.

4

WRITING UP THE
RESEARCH FINDINGS

IF THE methods section of an interview report ideally provides all relevant answers to the question "how do you know," the findings sections can be thought of as a set of interconnected responses to the reader's questions "what do you mean" and "what have you found out by interviewing people about this?" This chapter presents ways of optimizing the communication of the what-do-you-mean part of an interview study, so that interview papers and books can become as interesting and readable as possible, for only in this way can they have a chance of making a difference within the field of interest.

A very common problem in writing up qualitative interview findings concerns how to reduce or condense the often large amounts of data into a text that suits the standard formats of research communication (e.g. a journal article). In this chapter, I shall use this problem as a springboard for describing more generally how to report research findings in ways that are both compelling and rigorous. After dealing with the problem of data reduction, I discuss different ways of organizing the presentation of one's findings in terms of the macrostructure (i.e., the general argumentative or communicative drive of the research text) and also the microstructure (i.e., the crafting of concrete sentences and paragraphs) of the text.

I finally consider the role of theory in writing up the research findings and present two very different examples of excellent interview texts in this regard. If there is variety concerning how to write up the methodology of interview research, there is even more variety concerning how to write up the findings. This is as it should be, I believe, because the human conversational world, studied through qualitative interviewing, is rich and varied and cannot be captured adequately through one single formula. There is no golden standard for writing qualitative texts, but rather tips and tricks and rules of thumb, many of which I present below.

The Problem of Data Reduction

In his book on writing up qualitative research, Wolcott argues that the primary critical task in qualitative research "is not to accumulate all the data you can, but to 'can' (i.e., get rid of) much of the data you accumulate" (Wolcott, 2009, p. 39). From my experience, this applies to qualitative interviewing in particular. When interviewing, the problem is not to get data, for it is usually enjoyable and engaging to interview people about important features of their lives, so data collection often goes (almost too) smoothly. The problem arises afterwards, when the researcher has to reduce the often huge amounts of data into relevant bits that can be analyzed and written about, e.g. in a short journal article.

Kvale and Brinkmann refer to this problem as the 1,000-page question (Kvale & Brinkmann, 2008, p. 189): How shall I find a method to analyze the 1,000 pages of interview transcripts I have collected? After giving the reply that one should never do research in a way that results in 1,000 pages of transcripts (because it is too much to handle in a thorough manner, at least for a single researcher), they deconstruct the question by arguing (among other things) that there are no "methods" for analysis. Instead of "methods"—in the sense of procedures that will get the researcher quickly from A to B—there are interpretative stances and strategies for reading the materials. And these cannot be thought of as mechanical, but are deeply hermeneutic and depend on human experience and judgment.

This is not to say that there are no techniques for ordering, coding, and categorizing the empirical materials, or for looking for patterns or dynamic aspects of the data. There certainly are, and in Chapter 2, I described a number of inductive, deductive, and abductive ways of analyzing interview data. But the problem now is how to represent the huge amounts of data in a text that is quite possibly rather short.

One solution to this problem has been given by Peter Dahler-Larsen (2008) in a book on how to *display* qualitative data. According to Dahler-Larsen, the goal of displaying qualitative data clearly and transparently should be to demonstrate a chain of evidence for readers that links conclusions with data. Often, he finds, it is difficult for readers to follow how the researcher came from her data to her analyses and eventually to the findings, and this is a particular problem if one works with large, qualitative data sets. Displays are graphical ways of presenting qualitative data, e.g. in diagrams with arrows connecting different themes (if the researcher wishes to represent a specific relationship between different aspects of the field or phenomenon) or matrixes (if the researcher aims to show how bits of data have been categorized in various ways). The point about displays is that they are not just constructed as a way of interpreting data with categories constructed by the researcher, but that they literally put on display data in their primary form. Qualitative interviewers, perhaps because they use a language-based methodology, are often quite good at writing prose about their findings, but they rarely excel in building models or displays that demonstrate how the data they have analyzed are structured. This might be remedied by working with displays, and it thus represents a way of making the process of data analysis more visible to the reader.

Dahler-Larsen (2008) has invoked three rules for how to construct displays when communicating qualitative findings. He argues that displays should present data:

- Authentically.
- Inclusively.
- Transparently.

The first rule of authenticity means that data should appear in displays in their original and authentic forms. For qualitative interviewers, who work with transcripts as their data, this means that bits of the transcribed interviews should be included in the display. Not the researcher's interpretations of the interviewee statements, but the statements themselves should be displayed. Needless to say, the research report should also leave room for the researcher's interpretative interjections, but Dahler-Larsen's point is that these should not figure in the display.

The next rule about inclusion simply means that all data that are represented by a given category must be included in the display. And, if there are no bits of data that represent a specific category, the researcher should leave the field empty (e.g. in a matrix display). This can be a powerful way of communicating surprising absences in the interviews, as when Dahler-Larsen himself interviewed union representatives about democracy, and it turned out that the interviewees did not spontaneously use the word democracy or talk about democracy. So the field "democracy" was left empty in the display, which was a rhetorically effective way of informing the unions about their (failed) attempts at educating representatives in democratic processes.

The third rule of transparency says that it should be transparent or evident to the reader how the display has been constructed. In other words, there should be some sort of instruction to the reader about the premises that have been guiding in forming the display (e.g. concerning the two other rules, but also others). When working with displays, the constant aspiration is to enable the reader to look over the researcher's shoulder, especially concerning the (often unexplained) leap from raw data to conceptualization of the data, and finally to the construction of theoretical models of the phenomena studied.

I believe that the three rules can be useful, but they should be thought of as rules of thumb rather than static authorities about how to represent qualitative data in writing. Furthermore, two caveats should be mentioned: First, for large interview projects, especially if one works with rather broad categories (e.g. "democracy"), one might not attain much by representing *all* data bits about democracy (cf. the second rule) in their authentic entirety (cf. the first rule). As mathematician Norbert Wiener once said, the best model of a cat is a cat (and preferably the same cat). But if the goal is reducing large amounts of materials to things that can be handled and communicated effectively, one might need to reduce the cat to something less authentic than the cat itself! Thus, for some projects working with displays, the researcher may have to select a number of examples from the total empirical corpus that represents, say, democracy. Without necessarily buying into a quantitative research logic, no harm is done (quite the contrary) if one qualifies one's statements concerning generality. As Wolcott says about this matter:

> I think it judicious to examine, and, as appropriate, to qualify any and every statement a reader might perceive as a generalization that does not have a corresponding basis in fact. The phrase may get overworked, but scholarship does not suffer when a sentence begins with "As one villager commented..." rather than with "Villagers said..." (Wolcott, 2009, p. 27).

If one has just a few interviews, it is easy to write "As Fred said..." or "Fred and Joe both talked about...," which serves to contextualize the statements used (see below). And, for larger interview projects, one can write that "17 people out of 24 spontaneously mentioned anxiety when asked about..." Although this should not be interpreted in terms of statistical levels of significance, it might give the text a certain precision and face value.

The other caveat about displays concerns transparency. Even if this is a virtue in qualitative reports in standard cases, there are certain examples of excellent studies which are not particularly transparent. Notably, studies inspired by the literary turn in qualitative inquiry, e.g. within the area of autoethnographies or co-constructed narratives (Ellis & Berger, 2003) may convince the reader because of their aesthetic crafting or evocative powers and not because of explicit rules for displaying qualitative data.

Some qualitative researchers point to *resonance* as the most important sign of quality in a research text (e.g. Bochner, 2002). For if the reader is not *moved*—in some way—by what she reads, the text will not make a difference. How to write up findings with the aim of making the text resonate in the reader is discussed below, but Bochner argues that aesthetic qualities are indispensable in this regard, and these are improved when the researcher reports many concrete details, including her own feelings and doubts, communicates structurally complex narratives with honesty, credibility and vulnerability, relates to some process of human development in the research text, and is guided by ethical self-consciousness.

The literary tradition, in which Bochner works, does not normally use displays, so there are no rules without exceptions. In concluding on the use of displays, we can say that they are by no means compulsory in interview reports, but for researchers aiming to publish in outlets that are not open to experimental or more literary writing formats, they represent a useful tool for organizing data in a clear and pedagogical way for the reader. Needless to say, working with displays is not an automatic shortcut to a high-quality analysis. Displays are still constructed by researchers, which means that human judgment and interpretation continues to play a role, even if displays can make the organization of the end result of interpretation easier.

Presenting the Findings: The Macrostructure

I shall now move to more general issues about the macrostructure of the presentation of one's findings. Morse and colleagues claim that "every research project is a process of discovery (i.e., induction), the testing of hypotheses or conjectures (i.e., deduction), or the discovery of conjectures and the systematic testing of these conjectures within a single project (i.e., abduction)" (Morse, Niehaus, Wolfe & Wilkins, 2006, pp. 279–280). They argue that every research project has a primary *theoretical drive* (inductive, deductive, or abductive), an idea that also played a role in earlier chapters of this book. A research project may use a combination of these strategies or drives, but there is usually a main theoretical drive, which is normally chosen in the design phase of one's study (see Chapter 2).

When working out the macrostructure of one's write-up, it is useful to consider the theoretical drive that one has (hopefully) followed throughout the project: Was the project designed to discover something? In that case, the text should show how this discovery occurred and was facilitated by the research design and methodology. Was it designed to construct something? In that case, the text could take the form of an educational story, a story of *Bildung*, which shows how something new came into the world through the research project (e.g. new possibilities for action, new subject positions, or changed social practices). Or was the project designed to understand something? In that case, the findings should perhaps be written from the researcher's first-person perspective, enabling the reader to walk in the researcher's shoes, going through the same process of coming to understand something that was initially baffling.

Different Kinds of Stories

As a variant of this three-partite conception, Silverman (2000, p. 242) urges the researcher to report her findings based on one of three macrostructural models, conceived as different kinds of stories:

- The analytic story.
- The hypothesis story.
- The mystery story.

The analytic story is close to the *inductive* model of qualitative designs that I discussed in Chapter 2. The goal is to get to *findings* by analyzing a number of individual instances in order to arrive at more general knowledge, e.g. in the form of an overarching concept or category that explains what holds the individual instances together. The analytic concepts can either come before the analysis (through theory-driven coding), and are then be refined and revised in the inductive process of meeting the data, or through the analysis itself (data-driven coding) as in grounded theory. In any case, an analytic story convinces the reader when he or she can see how the researcher is moving from the particular to the general by means of analytic concepts.

When crafting an analytic story, Silverman encourages the researcher to pose the following questions to herself: What are the key concepts that I have used to get to my findings? (You may favorably revisit Figure 3.1 from the previous chapter to see that "findings" are a function of data, methodology, and theory, and never just one of these). How do the findings throw light on my concepts and the topics I have studied? What has become of my original research problem by working my way through the research process? A good analytic story begins with a clear statement of purpose, and is usually very explicit about its procedures of discovery (see the example below in Box 4.2).

The hypothesis story is (unsurprisingly) close to the *deductive* model of reasoning as described earlier. Its basic logic is shared with many quantitative studies: First, state your hypotheses; second, test them; third, discuss the implications (Silverman, 2000, p. 242). In this very strict form, the hypothesis story is unlikely to be of interest to interview researchers, who most often work with a much more dynamic and iterative research design, which should be reflected in the writings on findings. I have argued, however, that in a looser and more pragmatic sense, interview studies may indeed involve hypotheses or conjectures that are confronted with the empirical materials in a process of examining both (i.e. the hypothesis *and* the materials). A good hypothesis story in qualitative work convinces the reader by carefully working to avoid confirmation bias, by taking both positive and negative cases into account, and by systematically including and examining a variety of different interpretations instead of just sticking to one single reading (hypothesis) that is to be confirmed (or falsified).

Finally, the mystery story is close to my *abductive* model of scientific reasoning. When writing up the findings, the researcher will seek to take the reader through the same process from bewilderment through inquiry to coming to understand what was initially mysterious. As Alvesson and Kärreman have recently pointed out, good social science frequently springs from a breakdown ("I don't understand this"), coupled with a mystery (e.g. the framing of the breakdown as a riddle) and then a possible resolution of the riddle, e.g. based on a novel perspective on the matter that was confusing at first (Alvesson & Kärreman, 2011).

Alvesson and Kärreman's idea of qualitative research is thus breakdown-oriented, since it uses situations of breakdown (in understanding) productively to drive a research process forward (this is elaborated on in Brinkmann, 2012a). The main idea in breakdown-oriented research is that researchers should frame situations of breakdown as a mystery, which is a first step toward resolving the breakdown. When one has understood what the problem is, one has often already come a long way towards its resolution. Classically, this method is used by writers of crime fiction, who take the reader through the mystery before resolving it.

When breakdowns occur naturalistically, i.e., without the researcher intentionally trying to create them, there is an authentic opportunity to do qualitative inquiry with wider cultural significance. This is often where private troubles meet public concerns (Denzin, 2001). For interview researchers, breakdowns can occur naturalistically during the interviews, which is often a sign that something important is going on that should be analyzed and possibly reported as part of the findings (see Tanggaard, 2007, for an example). But when breakdowns do not simply happen, qualitative researchers may try to bring them about. Scott has outlined a number of general techniques in qualitative analyses of everyday life, some of which are directly breakdown-inducing (Scott, 2009, pp. 4–5). These techniques are:

• Make the familiar strange: In qualitative research interviews, people say many things that are common sense to conversationalists within a given culture. But imagine that you are an ethnographer from a different part of the world, who knows very little about the local cultural practices, including people's ways of describing experiences and accounting for their actions. Suddenly, many familiar things may become very interesting, and the material can be opened up in novel ways. The idea is to defamiliarize oneself from everyday occurrences in order to acknowledge their contingent natures (i.e., to acknowledge that they could have been different, provided that there had been other social practices and meaning horizons to construct them).

• Search for underlying rules, routines, and regularities: The episodes that make up qualitative interviews are not chaotic and anomic, but display an order that can be uncovered. This order is not causal, but normative. It concerns the *oughtness* of human conversational life (cf. Chapter 1). Discovering the rules that people follow (often without knowing it) in telling stories or describing events can be one way of experiencing a breakdown in understanding: Why these and not other rules?

• Challenge assumptions that are taken for granted. Social order is often revealed when the norms and rules (the webs of "oughtness") are broken, as Garfinkel (1967) demonstrated in his ethnomethodological studies. Breaking the rules in order to disclose them can be used as a strategy in interview studies (cf. the discussion of active and confronting interviews in Chapter 1), but this should be done with great care. Analytically, it may be done post hoc, as when the researcher analyzes the power relations that are at work in the ongoing production of the social world, in this case in research interviews (see Brinkmann & Kvale, 2005).

The mystery story can be chosen based on one of two ideas—either to communicate the experience of a breakdown, which the research process aimed to resolve (i.e. a naturalistic breakdown), or to report how a breakdown was induced analytically by the researcher in a way that resulted in a mystery that allowed the researcher to see the familiar in a new light. In both cases, the process can result in a very readable text if the mystery quality is kept in the findings section, eventually leading to resolving it or to accepting that the conversational world is inherently contradictory, disintegrative, and thus partly mysterious (Frosh, 2007). Perhaps qualitative researchers are sometimes too keen on integrating the bits and pieces of their data into larger explanatory wholes (whether narratives, discourses, categories, meaning units, or whatever), and are too unwilling to admit that not everything in our personal and social worlds suit such nice and linear writing formats.

Tales of the Field

In addition to the three kinds of stories that may provide the macrostructure to the presentations of findings, Van Maanen has, in his *Tales of the Field* (1988) developed a distinction between different kinds of tales, which has today become a classic. It may be worthwhile, also for qualitative interview studies, to consider Van Maanen's categories when deciding how to frame one's account. The three kinds of tales, which were developed from Van Maanen's own studies of police departments, are:

- The realistic tale.
- The confessional tale.
- The impressionistic tale.

In principle, the three kinds of tales cut across the distinction between the analytic, the hypothesis, and the mystery stories. One may write confessionally, for example, about how one's hypotheses about the social world came about, and how one went through a research process of testing them—or one may describe in a realistic manner how a breakdown occurred that led one to a mystery that was driving the research process forward.

The realistic tale is told in an unemotional voice, typically employing the third person stance, with the author being rather absent from the text. The research process is described as it happened, and the findings are presented, but without the researcher's subjectivity being highlighted. The epistemic virtues behind this tale are objectivity and reliability. Usually, realistic interview reports contain many quotes from the interviewees, which are meant to render the account authentic and objective. The main advantage of this kind of tale is the way it resonates with many people's ideas about what science is or should be, and it can therefore be a powerful way of communicating one's findings. But the downside is the real risk of clouding the researcher's role in the investigative process, which, paradoxically, is contradictory to the kind of objectivity that is otherwise the ideal in the rhetoric of realism.

The confessional tale is told in the first person, and is typically very personal and centered on the researcher as the instrument of knowing. Major aspects of a confessional tale may include the difficulties and dramas that the interviewer encountered in her work. Today, the autoethnographic approach, where the researcher reflects on his or her own experience in a given cultural situation, has been significant in making the confessional tale legitimate in many corners of the human and social sciences (about the role of autoethnography in relation to qualitative interviewing, see Ellis & Berger, 2003).

While the realistic tale focuses on the object of knowledge—the *known*—and the confessional tale focuses on the subject of knowledge—the *knower*—the third kind of tale, the impressionistic, seeks to bring together the knower and the known by highlighting the very activity of *knowing* itself. The impressionistic tale builds on the *how* of interviewing or fieldwork, rather than on the data or the researcher in isolation. Also, for Van Maanen, the impressionistic tale is reflexive, and can involve an innovative use of techniques and styles, as in impressionistic paintings, emphasizing the contingent and polyvocal aspects of the conversational reality that is studied through interviews. The impressionistic tale can favorably be coupled with the mystery story, articulating a learning process from initial bafflement to understanding of the social world.

Van Maanen's purpose in describing the different macrostructural styles of communicating findings is not to point to one true way of writing up qualitative research, but to alert researchers to the importance of rhetorical elements such as voice, style, and intended audience. Based on this knowledge, researchers are then able to choose the kind of tale that is most appropriate for what they want to say vis-à-vis the audience that they hope to reach.

In summing up on how to decide on the macrostructure of the write-up of one's findings, I find it useful to keep in mind the triangle depicted in Figure 3.1. For regardless of one's preferences and choices, it is important to present the findings in a way that takes all legs of the triangle into account. Data do not represent findings in themselves, for, as such, data are just what is there on the sound recorder or in the transcripts. Data become findings only when coupled with methodological and theoretical reflections, and all three of these should become visible in the findings section. In Box 4.2 below, I include an example of how to do this well.

Presenting the Findings: The Microstructure

In addition to working out the macrostructure of how to present the findings—deciding on the kind of story and tale one is going to tell—there are also lots of questions about the microstructure of one's presentation to consider. Some of these are general for qualitative writings, and some are specific to qualitative interviewing. I begin with some of the latter, before moving on to more general issues about how to write up qualitative findings on a microstructural level, i.e., concerning individual paragraphs and sentences.

Using Interview Quotes

The most common problem for interview researchers in relation to writing is how—and *how much*—to use excerpts from the interviews in the findings section. How (much) should interview quotes be used? Using displays, as I discussed above, might be helpful, but Kvale and Brinkmann (2008, pp. 279–281) have responded to the question in a different and more flexible way by developing a list of guidelines, which (as always) should not be thought of as universal and authoritative, but as rules of thumb that are useful in more than a few cases. They are presented in a reworked version below:

• The quotes used should be related to the general text: The researcher should provide a frame of reference for understanding the specific quotes and the interpretations given. The frames may relate to the life world of the participants or to the researcher's theoretical concepts and models, but it should be made clear what the quotes are related to in the general flow of the text.

• The quotes should be contextualized: The quotes are fragments of a more extensive interview context, which the researcher knows well (if she has conducted the interview herself), but which is unknown to the reader. It is helpful for the reader if the interview context of the quote is included. The question that prompted an answer, should normally be quoted, and the reader will then know whether a specific topic was introduced by the interviewer or by the interviewee, and possibly whether the question was in some way leading to a specific answer.

• The quotes should be interpreted: The researcher should state clearly what viewpoint a quote illuminates, proves, or disproves. It should not be up to the reader to guess why this specific statement was presented and what the researcher might have found so interesting about it. At the same time, the researcher's comments should not merely reproduce the quotes, perhaps in a slightly different wording, but should contribute some perspective on the material quoted. The latter is quite a widespread problem—that the researcher's interpretation simply rewords the interviewee's statement (which means that it is not really an interpretation)—often resulting in a text that is rather boring to read.

• There should be a balance between quotes and interpretation: The quotes should normally not make up more than half of the text in a chapter or article. When the interview quotes come from several interviewees, each with their particular style of expression, many quotes with few connecting comments and interpretations may result in a chaotic text.

• The quotes should in general be short: The maximum length of an interview quote is ordinarily half a page. After this length, the reader may lose interest, often because an interview passage contains several different dimensions, which makes it difficult for the reader to find a connecting thread. If longer passages are to be presented, they may be broken up and connected with the researcher's comments and interpretations. The exception to this rule is lively narrative interview passages, which may be read as stories of their own.

• Use only the best quote: If two or more interview passages illustrate the same point, then use only the best, e.g. that which is the most extensive, illuminating, and well-formulated statement. For documentation it is normally sufficient to mention how many other interviewees express the same viewpoints. If there are many different answers to a question among the participants, it will be useful to present several quotes, indicating the viewpoints they express. The idea of only using the best quote contrasts somewhat with Dahler-Larsen's inclusion rule for the construction of displays, but there is a difference between displays, as extensive visual expositions of data, and the researcher's more intensive use of selected quotes, which, of course, is allowed and usually necessary (since a display cannot interpret itself).

• Interview quotes should generally be rendered into a written style: Verbal transcriptions of oral speech, with repetitions, digressions, pauses, hmms, and the like are difficult to grasp when presented in a written form. Interview excerpts in a vernacular form, in particular in local dialects, also provide rough reading. To facilitate comprehension, the spontaneous oral speech should in most cases be rendered into a readable written textual form in the final report. The exception is when the linguistic form is important for the study, e.g. in so-called conversation analysis (see an example in Box 4.2).

• There should be a simple signature system for the editing of the quotes: The interview passages presented in the final report can be more or less edited. Sometimes, there is a need to do so for ethical reasons when names and places, which break with confidentiality, will have to be altered. In order for the reader to be able to understand the extent to which quotes have been edited, the principles for editing should be stated, and preferably with a simple list of signs for pauses, omissions, and the like.

General Issues in Findings Sections

Instead of stating positively how to develop the microstructure of one's findings section, it might also be helpful to discuss, more negatively, common weaknesses in interview reports. In a discussion of the use of autobiographic narratives as data (in applied linguistics studies specifically), Pavlenko (2007) highlights five major weaknesses that characterize many discussions of interview research findings. I believe that these may be generalized to many other kinds of interview studies (also outside linguistics), so they are worth mentioning here:

> The first is the lack of a theoretical premise, which makes in unclear where conceptual categories come from and how they relate to each other. The second is the lack of established procedure for matching of instances to categories. The third is the overreliance on repeated instances, which may lead analysts to overlook important events or themes that do not occur repeatedly or do not fit into pre-established schemes. The fourth is an exclusive focus on what is in the text, whereas what is excluded may potentially be as or even more informative. The fifth and perhaps the most problematic… is the lack of attention to ways in which storytellers use language to interpret experiences and position themselves as particular kinds of people. (Pavlenko, 2007, p. 166).

To this list, Talmy (2010) adds a sixth potential weakness concerning "issues of theoretical (in)compatibility, that is, when studies that are explicitly formulated with poststructuralist, social constructionist, and/or social practice theoretical frameworks adopt for their theory of interview a research instrument perspective." (p. 139).

As a remedy, reverting to a positive idiom, we may urge interview researchers, when they write up their research findings, to think about how to do the following:

• Explicate the theoretical premise of the analysis: Research findings do not come "unpolluted," free from theoretical concepts, so the research report needs to make clear how the conceptual categories (e.g. in a thematic analysis) were constructed.

• Describe how the individual instances (narratives, descriptions, accounts voiced by participants) were subsumed under more general categories in the analysis.

• Be careful about using the prevalence of an instance or theme as (the only) indication that the theme was important for the participants: One should not infer from the fact that there is a high degree of something in the material (in quantitative terms) that this something is therefore very important. This may be the case, but it has to be demonstrated with an argument that goes beyond counting instances.

• Pay attention not just to what interview participants talk about, but also to what they do *not* talk about: Absences are often as important as presences in human conversations (remember the example above about democracy among union representatives). Readers of interview reports will often want to know why some otherwise relevant theme was evaded by the participant (or researcher).

• Include reflections on the role of the interview as a social practice, even when the research interest concerns participants' *reports* of their experiences (see Chapter 1). The interview is always also a form of situated interaction that occasions the production of speech in particular ways, and an awareness of this should inform the analysis and the research findings.

• Beware of theoretical incompatibility: It is unfortunately very common to come across researchers who explicitly subscribe to a social constructionist epistemology, but at the same time are using the interview unreflectively as a "channel" to obtain data of participants' experiences (for example). If one chooses to combine techniques, procedures, and concepts from different philosophies and epistemologies, there should at least be a meta-theoretical or methodological discussion about the possible benefits (and legitimacy) of doing so (as argued by Talmy, 2010, p. 139).

With such pieces of advice in mind, the researcher can come a long way toward thinking about how to report the findings. This, however, does not in itself enable the researcher to write up her stories and descriptions. Since the seminal anthology on ethnographic writing, *Writing Culture* (Clifford & Marcus, 1986), a number of qualitative researchers have taken an interest in writing as a thinking tool, as a method of inquiry in its own right, for qualitative researchers (Harrington, 1997; Richardson & St.Pierre, 2005; Wolcott, 2009). In Box 4.1, I have summarized some of the useful tips to writers of qualitative texts that have emerged from some of these writers on writing.

Box 4.1 **Qualitative Writers on Qualitative Writing**

In this box, we shall revisit the writings of Kathy Charmaz and Laurel Richardson, whom I have already quoted on "writing as a method of inquiry" (a text coauthored by Bettie St. Pierre), and I also introduce Walt Harrington, who provides a perspective from intimate journalism. We begin with Richardson:

Richardson on Writing as a Method of Inquiry

Richardson makes clear that one becomes a good writer of qualitative findings only by practicing writing and reading exemplary texts (Richardson & St.Pierre, 2005). She encourages the researcher to put emphasis on four general aspects in communicating research findings: (1) The substantial contents of the analysis (what has been found out?), (2) aesthetic quality (aesthetics work not just as icing on the cake, but can enable precision and may also assist in expressing the polyvocal character of social life), (3) reflexivity (how has the researcher's subjectivity been both producer of and produced by the act of writing?), and (4) resonance (how is the reader affected by the text?).

Richardson also encourages researchers to do a number of more specific things. Some of the most important ones are:

- Join a writing group.
- Work through a creative writing guidebook.
- Enroll in a creative writing workshop.
- Use "writing up" field notes to expand one's writing vocabulary.
- Write an autobiography (e.g. about how one learned to write).
- Transform field notes into drama.
- Experiment with transforming an interview into a poem or a drama.

Like Richardson, who reports having been taught "not to write until I knew what I wanted to say" (Richardson & St.Pierre, 2005, p. 960), I believe that writing is a central way for qualitative interview researchers not just to report some findings, in the final instance, but also to experiment with analyses, different perspectives on the textual material, and ways of presenting, as a method of inquiry in its own right. Writing should thus be treated as an intrinsic part of the methodology of qualitative research—and not as a final "postscript" added on at the end.

Harrington on Intimate Journalism

Journalists can be some of the best interviewers and also the most acute observers of humans, perhaps because they make a living out of writing interesting stories about human lives. Much that goes by the name of journalism could also pass as qualitative research. Journalists do research, interviewing, observing, and they keep track of what they do—just as qualitative researchers. A good book on how to practice the craft of journalism is *Intimate Journalism: The Art and Craft of Reporting Everyday Life*, edited by Walt Harrington. In the opening essay, Harrington describes a number of basic writing techniques of intimate journalism, which are also useful to keep in mind for qualitative interviewers when they write up their findings (Harrington, 1997, pp. xx-xxi; some of the techniques are here paraphrased):

- Think, report, and write in scenes: Things never happen in a social and material vacuum, but social episodes unfold dramaturgically in specific settings. For qualitative interviewers, it is often helpful to describe the episodes of interviewing scenically, as a novelist would have done.
- Capture a narrator's voice and try to use it: Research communication is always narrated, but the narrator's voice is very often impersonal, which may be useful in some limited contexts, but in general, a story becomes more readable and interesting if it is articulated through a specific personal voice. This, obviously, can include the author's own voice in addition to the participants', and Wolcott adds that qualitative writers should always use the first person when writing descriptively (Wolcott, 2009, p. 17).
- Gather telling details from participants' lives: One should not simply describe what is said in an interview, but also note often how it is said, how people look while talking, how they are dressed and act etc. There is no clear line that defines what is relevant and what is not. Everything depends on the specific circumstances, knowledge interests, and the researcher's sensitivity.
- Gather real-life dialogue: As I argued in Chapter 1, social life is dialogical, and any utterance must be understood as a reply to what went before. It provides both life and credibility to the interview findings if real dialogues are communicated. That is, it is not just interviewee *answers* that are important, but also the conversational flow in which answers emerge and make sense, for they (the answers) are only what they are within this flow.

- Gather "interior" monologue: A research text can also communicate the researcher's own thoughts about the interviewees and what they say. The "interior" monologue can be communicated as when it occurred, during the interviews, or as an ongoing analytic commentary as in *Troubling the Angels* (Lather & Smithies, 1997), which was addressed in the previous chapter.

- Establish a time line that makes possible a narrative (with beginning, middle, and end): If social life is conversational and episodic, it revolves around beginnings, middles, and endings, and since narratives represent a fundamental human way of knowing (Bruner, 1991), it is often conducive to knowledge production *and* communication if the interview findings are reported as stories.

- Make the story resonate in readers: From a pragmatist perspective, research is significant when it facilitates change. So, one's story is only effective if it literally *moves* the reader. Those qualitative interview reports that are in fact read and used are very often those that are well written and which resonate in readers. A fantastic analysis, which no one understands or is moved by, might not be so fantastic after all.

- Don't make things up: Among numerous ethical considerations that are relevant, this one might be the most fundamental. In qualitative research, however, it is quite easy to add to or subtract from the reality that is studied. It is difficult for others to check if the researcher has made something up. If the interviewer herself is the research instrument, trustworthiness becomes a key moral virtue (see Brinkmann & Kvale, 2005).

Charmaz on Ethnographic Writing

In addition to advice from Richardson and Harrington, we have the piece by Charmaz, which I discussed in Box 3.2, but which ends with a number of relevant guidelines for ethnographic writing that are useful also for qualitative interviewers (once again, the points are paraphrased from her text and adapted to qualitative interviewing). According to Charmaz (1999, pp. 377–378), such writing should:

- Pull the reader in: The writer should invite the reader to stay with the story. This is done by providing the context of the story, by implying what might follow, and by reproducing the power of the interviewees' experience.
- Re-create experiential mood: The writing should keep the reader engaged, unify the scene and tighten the story, provide a view of the action or feeling with minimal distractions, distill experience to those narrative details that bring the scene to life, and finally "give priority to an effective story over efficient writing" (Charmaz, 1999, p. 377).
- Add surprise: The writer should show how unforeseen events pile on each other; observe when ordinary rules, values, and expectations are discarded, provide tension and surprise by recounting a predicament, and also add elements of surprise by revealing implicit meanings and rules, worldviews, or hidden social processes.
- Reconstruct ethnographic experience: The writer should do so by presenting images that resemble the experience, by striving to be faithful to the experience, and by showing rather than simply telling readers what is important.
- Create closure for the story: The writing should move forward by building tension, making the entire piece cohere, implying the closure from the beginning, and seeking to move the reader toward the conclusion through style, imagery, and voice.

Following guidelines, such as these from Richardson, Harrington, and Charmaz, should assist in enabling the researcher to write up findings in ways that are both compelling and precise. But time has come for me as well to show rather than tell, so the rest of this chapter will illustrate how excellent write-ups work by way of two examples. The exposition of the examples revolves around a key question about the role of theory in reporting qualitative findings.

The Role of Theory in Reporting Findings

If how to integrate interview quotes is the most commonly raised question about writing up findings based on qualitative interviewing, the role of theory is likely the second most frequent question:

How should one as a qualitative researcher balance theoretical and empirical issues in a findings section, especially in light of Figure 3.1, which indicates that both are (in the standard case) relevant in constituting the findings? What role should theory play? Very different ways of using theory exist, and I shall here present two examples of excellent interview reports that demonstrate diametrically opposed uses of theory: One is using theory in articulating the findings by telling an analytic story (Edwards, 2004), while the other is theory-free, but deeply evocative, written in a literary style, crafted rather more like a mystery story (Murakami, 2003).

Box 4.2 **Interview Findings on Racial Discourse**
···

When asked about an example of a good interview study, Alexa Hepburn, Reader in Conversation Analysis in the Department of Social Sciences at Loughborough University, UK (and coauthor of an important critique of conventional qualitative interview research to which we return in the next chapter, see Potter & Hepburn, 2005), answered: "If I had to pick one it would be Edwards, D. 2003: 'Analyzing racial discourse.'" Derek Edwards is Emeritus Professor of psychology at Loughborough and Hepburn's colleague, and he has been at the forefront of discursive psychology for many years.

Edwards' study is an illustration of how to work with discursive psychological tools in analyzing qualitative data (Edwards, 2004). It begins by outlining the main theoretical premises and "methodological stances" of discursive psychology. These are: First, "discursive psychologists avoid coming to conclusions that analysis can reveal people's true beliefs and attitudes." (p. 32). Instead, they look directly at talk as situated interaction and do not attempt to "see through" what people say to arrive at some truer psychological reality. Second, discursive psychologists focus on "contradictions, inconsistencies, and ambiguities" in human talk and (inter) action (p. 33) as important and interesting. They do not see such features as signs of flawed data. Third, they approach all talk as performative, and are committed to analyzing any kind of talk in terms of the situated actions it performs, even the most mundane kinds of talk. These is no separate "findings section" in Edwards' paper, but, using his methodological stances, he analyzes a number of extracts from interviews conducted in New Zealand, where racism appears as a theme. The findings are all informed by discourse analytic theory, but they are nonetheless rich in concrete empirical detail. Just to give one example, which also illustrates how many discursive psychologists prefer to transcribe interviews in a very detailed manner (from Edwards, 2004, p. 41):

1. R: It's *normally* that- Okay *that* argument gets put in that Maoris never get
2. the job's okay but you look. hh when they turn up for an interview
3. I: Yes
4. R: *What's* he wearing *how's* he sitting
5. I: Yeah
6. R: *How's* he talking > ya'know what I mean< an' there's no
7. *point* in having a receptionist that picks up a phone "Yeah
8. g'day 'ow are ya" ((strong New Zealand accent))
9. I: Ye:s (0.4) [mm mhm
10. R: [I mean they someone that is- (0.4) that is
11. gonna put their clients ar ea:se
12. I: Right (.) [Mm mhm
13. R: [You don't wanna *shop* a- a shop assistant who's *smelly*

"R" is the respondent and "I" is the interviewer, and the transcription contains information about how speakers emphasize certain words, how long the pauses are between words, when in the flow of words the next speaker interrupts etc. (see Jefferson, 1985, about these conventions for transcribing) The analysis follows immediately after the small excerpts, which are all analyzed very thoroughly.

In this case (just to give a glimpse of the analyses), Edwards argues that talk like this is used to sustain "a negative view of a group of people, while guarding against a disarming accusation of prejudice" by bringing off that view as rationally or accidentally arrived at (Edwards, 2004, p. 40). For example, he directs our attention to line 2, where the bit: "you look. hh when they turn up for an interview," appeals not only to what he calls scriptedness ("when they turn up for an interview"), but also to an event's experiential basis ("you look") (Edwards, 2004, p. 41). It formulates what anyone—and not just the speaker here—can (allegedly) see about Maoris as a general category. This, according to Edwards' analysis, is one way in which prejudice and racial discourse works. He also refers to a number of other microdiscursive mechanisms that are racializing, if not outright racist (e.g. how "factual claims" about minority groups are offered as only reluctantly arrived at, and how prejudice is performed—through talk—as something forced by the realities of no alternative).

Edwards also explains why interviews are methodologically relevant in this case (because it is difficult to obtain "naturally occurring talk" about everyday racism, which most discursive psychologists tend to prefer if at all available), and he reflects upon the limitations of the study, stating that there is no analysis of the cultural and historical background to the discourses mobilized by the participants in the interviews.

In her e-mail to me about the excellence of Edwards' study, Alexa Hepburn mentions a number of reasons for picking out this as exemplary:

- it draws on a broad understanding of conversation analysis, discursive psychology and ethnomethodology, which gives a clear and well supported set of tools for understanding interaction.
- it focuses directly on the activities done in the interview rather than putative mental states of participants.
- it works with a reasonably high quality transcript, capturing some features of delivery that could potentially change the meaning of utterances.
- it pays close attention to the interactional organization shown by that transcript.
- the interviews it uses were done with majority group members, avoiding the common (and potentially oppressive) problem of focusing on minority group members' talk and producing it as evidence of what they "really think/feel."

- the interviews were specifically designed to be conversational and at times argumentative. (E-mail communication August 11, 2011).

As the example and Hepburn's reasons for highlighting it testify, Edwards' text illustrates very well how theory can lead to qualitative findings, which necessitates integrating the theoretical machinery into an exposition of the findings themselves. Edwards does this in a lucid manner, and his paper is a nice example of how findings can emerge from the data-methodology-theory triangle (cf. Figure 3.1). His form of discursive psychology definitely forms a "package" that encompasses all three legs of the triangle.

I shall now contrast Edwards' theory-rich account of findings with a theory-free (at least in terms of social science theory) account, represented by an interview study by Haruki Murakami.

Box 4.3 **Interview Findings on the Tokyo Gas Attack**

When asked about examples of excellent qualitative interview studies, critical psychologist and qualitative methodologist Ian Parker (see e.g. Parker, 2005) kindly answered by pointing to an interview book by the famous Japanese novelist Haruki Murakami, entitled *Underground: The Tokyo Gas Attack and the Japanese Psyche*. In an e-mail, Parker said: "This extraordinary book is the best example of what researchers should aim at in qualitative interviewing." As someone who had read Murakami's books of fiction with great pleasure, I was thrilled to discover that he had also done an interview book. The purpose of the book is to tell the story of the terrorist attack (using Sarin gas), by the infamous Aum Shinrikyo cult, which hit the Tokyo underground system on March 20, 1995. The book is divided into two parts. The first part consists of interviews with surviving victims, while the second part (added a year later for the second edition) is based on interviews with members and ex-members of the cult.

Parker continues in his e-mail: "I can use this book to draw attention to some "signs of quality," as you put it, in qualitative interviewing.

Murakami briefly describes the methodological process of interviewing his participants in the "preface" to the book, and succeeds in making that description of the process into part of a narrative of the work, and he then explores reflexive aspects of the work, his own position as interviewer, in the "afterword."

The work has a literary quality in which it flows in its narrative as if it were a novel, in fact as if it were a novel written by Haruki Murakami, and in this way it brings to life the accounts gathered in the interviews to honor the different experiences of participants.

The study embeds the individual interviews in an account of the cultural-historical context in which the event happened, and so enables the interviews to throw new light on the event so that we understand something that concerns us all better." (E-mail communication August 20, 2011).

It is impossible to do justice to Murakami's study with a short quotation, but let me exemplify anyway how he writes as an interview researcher. In the following excerpt, he interviews Shizuko Akashi (a pseudonym), a 31-year-old woman, at the hospital where she is being treated because of brain damage that was caused by the gas attack; her brother is also present. Shizuko remembers nothing before the attack:

"Her brother slowly pushes Shizuko's wheelchair out into the lounge area. She's petite, with hair cut short at the fringe. She resembles her brother. Her complexion is good, her eyes slightly glazed as if she has only just woken up. If it wasn't for the plastic tube coming from her nose, she probably wouldn't look handicapped.

Neither eye is fully open, but there is a glint to them—deep in the pupils; a gleam that led me beyond her external appearance to see an inner something that was not in pain.

'Hello,' I say.

'Hello,' says Shizuko, though it sounds more like *ehh-who*.

I introduce myself briefly, with some help from her brother.

Shuzuko nods. She has been told in advance I was coming,

'Ask her anything you want,' says Tatsuo [Shuzuko's brother].

I'm at a loss. What on earth can I say?

'Who cuts your hair for you?' is my first question.

'Nurse,' comes the answer, or more accurately, *uh-errff*, though in context the word is easy enough to guess. She responds quickly, without hesitation. Her mind is there, turning over at high speed in her head, only her tongue and jaws can't keep pace. For a while at first Shizuko is nervous, a little shy in front of me. Not that I could tell, but to Tatsuo the difference is obvious. 'What's with you today? Why so shy?' he kids her, but really, when I think about it, what young woman wouldn't be shy about meeting someone for the first time and not looking her healthy best? And if the truth be known, I'm a little nervous myself.

Prior to the interview, Tatsuo had talked to Shizuko about me. 'Mr Murakami, the novelist, says he want to write about you Shizuko, in a book. What do you think about that? Is it all right with you? Is it okay if your brother tells him about you? Can he come here to meet you?'

Shizuko answered straight away, 'Yes.'

Talking with her, the first thing I notice is her decisive 'Yes' and 'No,' the speed with which she judges things. She readily made up her mind about most things, hardly ever hesitating.

I brought her yellow flowers in a small vase. A color full of life. Sadly, however, Shizuko can't see them. She can only make things out in very bright sunlight. She made a small motion with her head and said, '*Uann-eyhh* [Can't tell].' I just hope that some of the warmth they brought to the room—to my eyes at least—rubs off atmospherically on her." (Murakami, 2003, pp. 86–87).

We here witness an interviewer, who reports his interview in a literary style, interjecting his own thoughts and doubts between the sentences, but it is not fiction. Murakami makes clear that all interview sessions (each lasting between one and four hours—and 60 victims and eight cult members were interviewed) were recorded and transcribed. In the process of writing up, Murakami sent drafts to the interviewees, "for fact-checking," and "Almost everyone asked for some changes or cuts, and I complied." (Murakami, 2003, p. 5). Murakami has many ethical considerations throughout the book, seeking in particular "to avoid any exploitative mass-media scenario" (p. 5).

The book is written without social science theorizing, but certainly not without researcher reflexivity or critical thinking. And, because of the extensive reporting of the interview dialogues, the reader can follow the interviewer's way of working at first hand, and we learn, for example, that Murakami's style of interviewing would often be a variant of what I called an actively confronting style in the first chapter: "When I didn't understand something," he explains in a "methodological" preface to the book's part two, "I just went ahead and exposed my ignorance; when I thought that most people would not accept a certain viewpoint, I challenged it. 'It might hold a certain logic,' I'd say, 'but your average person wouldn't buy it.'" (Murakami, 2003, p. 215).

Few of the interview studies that I have read are as intriguing as Murakami's. What is it that works so well in his book? Ian Parker explains in his e-mail how he finds that *Underground* avoids three shortcomings that are otherwise very widespread in much qualitative research interviewing:

1) Often research studies describe their 'methodology' in dry boring terms that deaden the response of the reader instead of inviting the reader into the narrative. (2) They often reduce the interview accounts to a string of quotes mixed with jargonised 'interpretations' that mischaracterise what was really said, and what the narrative was really about. (3) They often attempt to focus on a particular account, losing sight of the reasons why research is carried out, and we end up learning nothing of any use beyond the particularity of the interview." (E-mail communication August 20, 2011; the numbers in parentheses are added on by me, SB).

Against these shortcomings, Murakami's book, in quite a non-theoretical manner, succeeds in making methodology appealing, in reporting a number of remarkable interviews, and in situating the interviews in a larger cultural context (seeking to understand "the Japanese psyche" through this tragic event).

Conclusions

In this chapter, I have provided different theoretical and practical tools which are meant to assist researchers in writing up their findings. We began with the problem of how to reduce a large amount of data to something that can be communicated in a short journal article or book chapter. One solution was described in some detail, viz. working with displays as a way of modeling data and relationships within data. This, however, does not remove a need for writing more analytically or interpretively about one's research in the findings section. Concerning how to organize the findings, I distinguished between macrostructural issues, suggesting different kinds of stories and tales to organize the presentation of findings, and microstructural issues, related to the concrete crafting of sentences and paragraphs. Regarding the latter, I included tips and tricks from great writers on qualitative writing.

Finally, I provided two examples of how to report interview findings—texts by Derek Edwards and Haruki Murakami—the first of which was analytical, informed by theory, and based on an (explicit) idea (from discursive psychology) of the interview as a social practice that is constitutive of the talk it generates (cf. Table 1 in this book's first chapter). Edwards' text thus treated interviewee talk as *accounts*, occasioned by the situations in which they occurred. Murakami's interview book is very different: It is evocative, uses techniques from literature, and is based on an (implicit) idea of the interview as a research instrument that is used to collect stories of people's experiences. Without thematizing it, Murakami thus approaches interviewee talk as *reports* of past events, and comes close to a form of oral history (Leavy, 2011). Edwards' text articulates an analytical story, while Murakami's conveys more of a mystery story, literally working on the basis of a (very tragic) breakdown in social life (the Tokyo gas attack).

The fact that interview studies can be as diverse as Edwards' and Murakami's, but still, in their different ways, be exceptionally good and thought-provoking, testifies to the heterogeneous conversational world of humans, and is proof of the rich possibilities of using interviews for knowledge-producing purposes. In the next and final chapter, we shall turn to the question of quality—what makes an interview study good?—and also to some of the problems that critics see in qualitative interviewing as conventionally practiced.

5

DISCUSSION OF
QUALITATIVE
INTERVIEWING

IN PREVIOUS chapters, we have looked at qualitative interviewing, not as one specific method, but as a set of different practices that all employ conversations for knowledge-producing purposes (Chapter 1). Current conceptions of interviewing draw upon many different historical sources, some of which frame the interview as a research instrument that enables the telling of past experiences, while others conceive of the interview as a site for confrontations and negotiations of meaning.

In line with the idea that qualitative interviews are, and should be, heterogeneous, we saw in Chapter 2 that a number of different approaches to research design exist in the literature on qualitative interviewing. Some aim for discovery, others for understanding, while a few have the explicit aim of constructing something that was not there before (e.g. a new social practice). Furthermore, designs can be mainly inductive, deductive, or abductive. In spite of the varied landscape of qualitative interviewing, I presented a generic way of thinking about design that should help researchers get an overview of an entire research process.

In the two chapters that followed, the focus changed to the writing up of research. Chapter 3 focused on how to write up the methods section, and Chapter 4 concentrated on the research findings. In some interview reports, this distinction is quite artificial and does not speak to how research is actually communicated (for example, if one decides to integrate the methodological descriptions into one' general research narrative). In other cases, it is considered standard practice to divide one's research report (and one's research process as such) into these stages. Again, I did not present One True Way of writing up qualitative interview research, but offered something like a menu of different options that are suitable for different *purposes* (i.e., research interests), *projects* (i.e., in relation to particular institutional contexts with their specific traditions), and *preferences* (i.e., related to who you are as a researcher and writer). A good interview study will often balance and speak to all three aspects—the purpose of the study, the project, and the institutional traditions behind it, and the preferences of the person.

In this concluding Chapter 5, I will do two things: First, I will present some points of criticism that are often raised against qualitative interviewing. Some of these are raised from people outside the world of qualitative research as such, while others are raised by insiders to qualitative inquiry. I consider each in turn. Second, I describe and discuss different strategies for evaluating qualitative interview research. How should readers of interview studies assess what they read? Is it possible to articulate criteria for quality in relation to interviewing, and if so, which ones are relevant?

Problems in Qualitative Interviewing: External Critiques

I will organize this section as a list of objections that used to be voiced, almost as an automatic reaction, in hostile opposition to qualitative research in general, and sometimes to qualitative interviewing in particular, as qualitative interviewing probably represents the most widespread approach to qualitative work. Today, fortunately, the situation has changed for the better, so that qualitative inquiry—at least in many disciplines—does not have to be defensive, constantly working under the threat of being attacked. But still, the objections listed here have not disappeared, so they deserve to be rehearsed and rebutted, if only in a few words.

Qualitative Research Is Not a Valid Scientific Method

Few people will say explicitly today that qualitative interviewing is unscientific because it does not involve numbers and statistics as part of its scientific apparatus. However, if we look at the current "audit culture," and notice the research projects that receive most of the large grants, we definitely witness a move towards so-called "evidence-based" practice in the professions (typically involving randomized, controlled trials as research methodology) (Kvale, 2008). There has been a move from philosophical positivism as a prime threat to qualitative research towards something that could be called "bureaucratic" or "economic" positivism. With a background in biomedicine, the Cochrane movement (an international agency that monitors the effectiveness of medial treatments) has in particular developed an evidence hierarchy, which has placed randomized controlled experiments as "the gold standard," and expert opinion, as well as qualitative research, at the bottom level of evidence. These strict criteria of evidence *may* be adequate for some parts of biomedical research. However, when they are extrapolated to other forms of research, they too often result in a "politics of evidence" (Morse, 2006), where qualitative research in general becomes marginalized.

The whole "what works" agenda thus threatens to marginalize qualitative research that does not study *what* works, but rather *how* something works. In this sense, however, qualitative research cannot be dispensed with. It remains fundamental even in an audit culture (where it is often sadly forgotten), since we must know what the "what" is that works—and *how*. Qualitative studies remain relevant for practitioners in particular, who do not really know what to do with a piece of information like "In 67 percent of cases, intervention X is likely to have a beneficial effect." Research seeking to build an evidence base is mainly for policy makers, and not for practitioners, who will often benefit much more from a good case description or narrative that can inspire them to act in their work, than from information about statistical averages.

The postulate that valid sciences necessarily use numbers and statistics could be countered with numerous examples from biology, paleontology, or anatomy that demonstrate that great scientific discoveries have been made without statistics. Harvey's discovery that the heart is a pump did not involve numbers or statistics, but careful descriptions and interpretations of the functioning of this vital organ. *Real* sciences, it can even be argued, do not need statistics to demonstrate effects; and as Rom Harré has said about qualitative psychology, "It is the qualitative techniques and the metaphysical presumptions that back them that come much closer [in comparison with mainstream quantitative psychology] to meeting the ideals of the natural sciences." (Harré, 2004, p. 4). Qualitative analysis is a major subfield in chemistry; biologists do fieldwork and case studies; and much of the science of physiology is purely descriptive. This, clearly, does not render these sciences invalid—so why should the qualitative parts of the human and social sciences be considered invalid? I doubt that anyone would question, for example, that the study by Edwards (2004) on racial discourse demonstrates a valid scientific approach in spite of the lack of statistics (see Box 4.2). Edwards has found a number of racializing mechanisms in human talk that are widespread, and the study is convincing not because of *how many* instances Edwards has analyzed, but because of *how well* he proceeds.

Qualitative Interviewing Relies on Subjectivity and Thus Cannot Give Us Objective Knowledge

This objection should be met with a question: "What do you mean by *objective* knowledge?" If objective knowledge means knowledge that reflects its subject matter, it seems to be uncontroversial that qualitative interviewing can give us just that. For interviews seem uniquely capable of capturing central aspects of human conversational processes, self-understandings, and ways of talking, reasoning, and describing past experiences. We should always use the methods of inquiry that are adequate to the subject matter we are interested in, and when the subject matter is the conversational reality that I depicted in Chapter 1, I doubt that any method can claim objectivity to a greater extent than qualitative interviewing.

Kvale and Brinkmann (2008, pp. 242–244) discuss many different meanings of the concept "objectivity" and conclude that qualitative interviewing can in fact be an objective method according to all of these. It is true that interviewing relies on subjectivity—the researcher herself is the research instrument, as I have put it in this book—but it is certainly possible to strive for objectivity about subjectivity, at least to some extent, which is a process of researcher reflexivity (see Chapter 3). Objectivity is an ideal and not something given, and as such, it is never reached in a pure form, but the fact that a perfectly aseptic environment is in principle unattainable doesn't mean that one should conduct surgery in a sewer, to paraphrase Clifford Geertz (1973, p. 30). Researchers working with interviews can strive to avoid bias and demonstrate eloquent craftsmanship, thus attaining a degree of objectivity that compares easily with other methods. I would argue that most of the interview studies that I have referred to in this book live up to an ideal of objectivity, even those (or perhaps *especially* those), like Wacquant's (1995) that reconstruct a first person perspective on a reflexive basis, and thereby demonstrate that one may strive for objectivity about subjectivity (see Box 2.3).

Qualitative Interviewing Involves Human Judgment and Thus Lacks Reliability

It is true that interviews depend on the specific meetings between interviewer and interviewee, and that they cannot be repeated in the same form with other people involved. It is also true that different analysts of the same empirical interview materials will interpret these interviews in different ways. These truisms have been invoked by people outside qualitative research to argue that qualitative interviewing is therefore not reliable as a scientific method; the human factor is too momentous, it is said.

In response, one can say that in qualitative interviewing, all there *is* is the human factor. There would not be anything to analyze, were it not for the human factor—human beings talking, interacting, understanding (or not), and interpreting each other— but this does not mean that analyses and interpretations cannot be rationally discussed and assessed. Very often, researchers do in fact agree about how talk or conversational processes should be interpreted. When they do not, it is not necessarily because of "low reliability," but it may stem from the inherently polyvocal and heterogeneous reality that is studied in qualitative inquiry.

That said, it is indeed possible to strive for a high degree of reliability in qualitative interviewing, if it is relevant to do so. One can have independent coders, for example, who code the same materials, and it is then possible to calculate inter-coder-reliability, if one should wish to do so. For some projects, this can be relevant, but, in most cases, it will be too expensive (and often too little will result from this practice). If reliability means that different people can see the same thing in the material, then qualitative interviewing can certainly be reliable. The study by Morse and Mitcham, for example, which I addressed in Box 2.1, contradicts the objection that qualitative interview research cannot be reliable (Morse & Mitcham, 1998). The way the researchers carefully considered different analytic conjectures, and took negative cases into account, makes it very likely that other analysts would reach similar conclusions.

Qualitative Interviewing Is Normally Based on A Few Cases and Thus Cannot Be Generalized

Finally, we come to the question of generalizability, which, I believe, is the most common external objection voiced against interview research. Generalizability is about the extent to which findings in one context (e.g. interviews with 10 middle-aged, homosexual men in London) can be transferred to other contexts (e.g. to all homosexual men in London, or in the UK, or in the West, etc.). Qualitative studies cannot, like quantitative studies, demonstrate generalizability statistically (by invoking a significance level, for example), but must employ some form of analytic generalization (Kvale & Brinkmann, 2008). This rests on theoretical understanding of the subject matter, and is also found in the natural sciences. Harvey could generalize from one heart to all hearts (that they are pumps), not based on any statistical tests, but rather on the theoretical idea that human organs function similarly in similar living bodies. Analogously, phenomenologists will sometimes be able to generalize about essential structures of human experience, and conversation analysts will sometimes be able to generalize about core features of human talk. Generalization rests to a large extent on a theoretical understanding of the subject matter.

One has probably done a good job, as a qualitative researcher, when the question "But can this be generalized?" does not even arise. In that case, people will simply recognize a description or a story as significant—either because it succeeds in demonstrating something that is typical (but perhaps was so obvious that no one has described it as such before), or because it describes something that is novel: Perhaps the researcher has made a genuine discovery. Obviously, this also happens in the natural sciences. When Syunzo Kawamura and colleagues discovered in the 1950s that certain monkeys on the Kyushu island in Japan teach the younger members of the troop to wash potatoes before eating them, it was revolutionary, because it falsified the idea that only humans have "culture" in the sense of knowledge that is not transmitted genetically but through education (Kawamura, 1959). No one who has read about the discovery will say: "But this cannot be science, because it does not generalize to all monkeys!" Likewise, most people who read Wacquant will not ask if his descriptions can be generalized to all boxers, or ask Morse and Mitcham if their findings can be generalized to all burn patients, or confront Edwards with the question if his analysis generalizes to all forms of racist talk. These questions are somehow off the mark, because the studies have such high face value and convince the reader because of the researchers' craftsmanship.

In ending the discussions (and, I hope, rebuttals) of the external objections, I will raise the question whether it would be preferable simply to discard the terms validity, objectivity, reliability, and generalizability altogether for qualitative interviewers. Quite a few qualitative researchers have suggested this strategy and argued that qualitative researchers should develop their own concepts, mapping the specific virtues that characterize excellent qualitative inquiry. When reading Murakami's interview book, for example, one is struck by the power of the prose, the precise descriptions, and the moving stories, and not by the degree of objectivity, reliability, or generalizability.

Although I am all in favor of experimenting with new concepts to describe and assess our practices, I believe that there is also value in sticking to these old ones. Doing so will, first, enable qualitative researchers to engage in dialogue about their work with people from other research traditions. Second, it will unite qualitative researchers with the great canon of scientists, many of whom were, by today's standards, qualitative researchers. This, I believe, is something that has great rhetorical value if qualitative researchers are to convince funding agencies and other powerful institutions in the current audit culture. Charles Darwin, arguably among the most influential scientists of all times, was a qualitative researcher, was he not? He described and analyzed the qualities of what he saw and informed his analyses with innovative theoretical thinking. If one browses through a book by Darwin to look for his statistics, one will be disappointed. Well, if Darwin needed qualitative research, perhaps so do we?

My suggestion is thus that qualitative interviewers include reflections on validity, objectivity, reliability, and generalizability in their studies and research reports, albeit in ways that respect the unique practices of qualitative research. The concepts should not be discarded, but accommodated to qualitative inquiry. What it means to generalize, for example, is wholly different for a qualitative interviewer in comparison with her quantitative colleagues. Understanding these differences (and also the similarities) demands some schooling in philosophy of science, and preferably also knowledge of different scientific traditions and disciplines.

Problems in Qualitative Interviewing: Internal Critiques

I shall now move from traditional, and rather sweeping, external critiques of qualitative interviewing to a range of objections that have recently been voiced by insiders to qualitative inquiry. Rather than constructing another straw man to represent the critical voice, I shall refer to a recent critical commentary on qualitative interviewing. In an influential paper, Jonathan Potter and Alexa Hepburn (who, as discursive psychologists, are certainly insiders to qualitative inquiry) raise a number of concerns about qualitative interviews in psychology (Potter & Hepburn, 2005). However, I believe that their points pertain to qualitative interviewing in general.

Their paper is written from the premise that qualitative interviewing has become the method of choice in modern qualitative psychology (Potter & Hepburn, 2005, p. 282). I believe that this is a fair judgment. The authors do not wish to exorcise interviews from qualitative inquiry, but they argue that interviews should always be justified in a concrete research project by the object of inquiry. This, as I argued in Chapter 1, is a step that is too often by-passed. The choice to do interviews is simply taken for granted in too many research projects.

Potter and Hepburn distinguish between contingent and necessary problems in qualitative interviewing. The contingent ones are widespread, but are not a necessary feature of doing interview research. That is, they can be fixed, sometimes quite easily (Potter & Hepburn, 2005, p. 285). These problems concern:

- The deletion of the interviewer.
- The conventions for representing interaction.
- The specificity of observations.
- The unavailability of the interview set-up.
- The failure to consider interviews as interaction.

I shall address each in turn.

The deletion of the interviewer in interview reports (e.g. when quoting from the interviews) is a problem, because the interviewee's talk is then being taken out of context (Potter & Hepburn, 2005, p. 285), reported almost as if it fell from the sky, unoccasioned by any human relationships or interests. Most, if not all, qualitative paradigms build on an idea of contextuality: that the phenomena (human experience, action, or discourse) studied by the human and social sciences are what they are only within some context. Taken out of context, they no longer are what they were, when they were contextually produced. Thus, it is ironic that so many interview researchers, who otherwise subscribe to different contextual philosophies, continue to take interviewee statements out of their contexts when presenting them in reports. Fortunately, this can be remedied by including the interactional flow with questions and responses in the interview analysis and report (and we saw two excellent examples of this in the previous chapter). Doing so will also be a remedy against the last problem stated (the failure to consider interviews as interaction), for it will force analysts to consider the role played by the interactional process in producing the kind of talk that is subsequently analyzed.

The second point can be countered by using a style of transcription that captures several elements of talk that are interactionally relevant, such as vocal emphasis, pauses in seconds, in-breaths and out-breaths, pitch, overlapping speech etc. An example of this was discussed in Box 4.2. When doing conversation analysis, which involves a close reading of how the form of interaction works together with and affects the contents of what is said, it is very relevant to carefully transcribe these features of talk. But in my view, it is less relevant for many other projects, and I doubt that Murakami's book (discussed in Box 4.3) would have been improved had it employed conversation analytic transcriptions. As Parker (2005) has argued, the conversation analytic rules sometimes lead to a "textual empiricism," where one is not allowed to say anything about the phenomenon that is not directly visible in the transcription, and this is of little value in most qualitative research projects. So, I would qualify Potter and Hepburn's critique on this point and say that for those projects that depend on some form of interaction analysis, interaction should be closely and carefully represented, while for others, it may be less relevant. In all cases, however, one's choice should be backed by good reasons.

The third point mentioned above concerns how claims about interviews are substantiated in qualitative analyses. According to Potter and Hepburn, a key challenge in analyzing interviews "is to show how your claims can account for the specifics of talk, not just its broad themes." (Potter & Hepburn, 2005, p. 289). I have already touched upon this when discussing the relationship between the empirical materials and one's analytic interpretations in the previous chapter. One should show concretely what it is in the materials that warrants a specific interpretation and why. A simple step toward a solution can be to work with line numbers in the transcription and be careful to refer to these in one's interpretations.

Finally, the fourth contingent problem is about the interview set-up not being sufficiently described: How were the participants recruited? What categories were invoked in attracting them to the research project? Recreational drug user? Or drug addicts? And what was the task understanding communicated to the participants? (Potter & Hepburn, 2005, p. 290). These important features of the whole practice of interviewing are often not reported or discussed. Again, this problem can be remedied by being careful in reporting these factors, and, when relevant, taking them into account in the analysis.

As we have seen solutions are available for the five contingent problems pointed out by Potter and Hepburn. My pragmatic stance is that they are not always problematic, but only in relation to specific research interests. However, Potter and Hepburn also cite what they believe are four *necessary* problems, which are not so easily solved (Potter & Hepburn, 2005, p. 291). These concern:

- The flooding of interviews with social science agendas and categories.
- The complex and varying positionings of interviewer and interviewee.
- The possible stake and interest of interviewer and interviewee.
- A predominance of cognitive and individualist interpretations.

The first point is about how the construction of interview questions invites participants into specific social science agendas that may not be important to interviewees in their everyday lives. However, I believe that this only becomes a problem if one approaches interviews as channels through which participants' experiences can flow, unmediated by the way the researcher constitutes the research situation. As I have argued throughout this book, the social practice of interviewing always mediates (rather than *determines*) the talk that goes on between the conversationalists, and this is taken into account in the best interview studies.

Something similar is the case with the second point, which I addressed in Chapter 1 through Briggs (2007), who has argued that interviews imply a specific "field of communicability" (p. 556) that involves different roles, positions, relations, and forms of agency. These are a function of the interview as a social practice, and can hardly be eliminated (which is probably why Potter and Hepburn refer to this as a necessary problem), but, again, it is only a problem if it remains unacknowledged in the analysis.

The third problem (of stake and interest) has been raised by discursive psychologists, who claim that people may always answer questions based on particular interests (which are often more complex than "telling the truth," for example). This also pertains to interviews, where participants often have a stake in the categories to which they are assigned and in the themes they are talking about. Not just interviewees, but also interviewers have something at stake in the interaction, and sometimes a lot. Interviewers, as Potter and Hepburn note, are often responsible for doing a research project, e.g. a Ph.D., which means that they take an interest not only in the phenomenon they are studying but also in how interviewees address it in their talk (in that sense, interviews are instrumental conversations, set up according to the researcher's agenda, as I discussed in Chapter 1). Few interview reports include in the analysis how the interviewer/researcher displays agreement or disagreement with the interviewee, for example, thereby co-constructing the way the phenomenon is addressed.

I agree with Potter and Hepburn that this is a necessary problem, because people cannot *not* have something at stake in interview encounters, but the problem *can* be handled by approaching it analytically, as something to be taken into account. The problem of stake is part of the human condition, and is not unique to qualitative interviewing. There is no way to solve it (this would eliminate the dynamism of human conversations), so instead it should be approached as an interesting feature that is relevant to look at when analyzing conversations. It is in principle always possible to interpret people's talk as "sincere" and/or as "strategic," and one cannot know in advance what the most convincing interpretation will be.

Finally, Potter and Hepburn argue that some form of cognitivism (the questionable idea that psychological processes uniquely take place "in the mind" of individuals) is reproduced in and through the practice of interviewing. Although this is a real risk, I believe that the interview projects that I have singled out as exemplary in this book (e.g. in the various boxes) demonstrate that it need not be the case. Interviews, when analyzed properly, can lead to insights about social problems and health issues, for example, that are not reduced (or reducible) to individual cognitions. It all depends on *how* one approaches the analysis of interviews. This leads to the next section on quality in qualitative interview projects.

Quality in Qualitative Interviewing

The question about quality in qualitative research has been hotly debated (Bochner, 2002; Brinkmann, 2007b; Parker, 2004). There is today a huge literature on quality and different criteria for how to assess quality, probably because of the many-sidedness and multi-paradigmatic nature of qualitative inquiry. Some commentators believe that we should simply use the (alleged) universal criteria of validity, reliability, generalizability, and objectivity that were discussed above. Others argue that each paradigm needs its own set of criteria, which means that a good phenomenological analysis is different from a good post-structural analysis, which is different from... If paradigms are indeed incommensurable, as Thomas Kuhn (1970) famously argued, then this is perhaps a sensible suggestion. The problem, however, is that Kuhn cannot be used to back this idea. He would likely say that, according to his definition of a paradigm, there are as yet no paradigms in the human and social sciences, but only pre-paradigmatic confusion, and also that it would easily lead to a Babel-like situation with numerous tribes that would not be able to communicate with each other. (On one reading, alas, this is how the situation is today).

Another current voice in qualitative inquiry simply claims that we could and should do without quality criteria altogether—we should simply let the thousand flowers bloom. I believe that this idea is both true and false. From my point of view (which is grounded in a form of generous and non-dogmatic pragmatism), it is true that we should in principle listen to everyone and not exclude people because they work according to quality criteria that we are not familiar with. But the idea is false in the sense that we probably never can escape criteria, at least not the ones that are implicit in our judgments, or our Gadamerian "prejudices," so it is better to spell them out and discuss them openly.

Responding to an email from me about quality in research interviewing, Martin Packer, author of *The Science of Qualitative Research* (2011) and editor of *Qualitative Research in Psychology*, gave a nice answer that I have been permitted to quote here:

Quality in research interviewing? That's tricky, but I guess I'd say (1) awareness on the part of the researcher that what they hear was crafted for their ears, (2) attention to the details of the language, with emphasis on its pragmatics, (3) an avoidance of claiming to have "the" reading, the final word. The problems would be the opposite: (1) treating the interview as an expression of the speaker's subjectivity or experience and failing to take into account the circumstances of its production, (2) ignoring the language; treating it as transparent, or as a container (and that includes most kinds of coding); (3) presenting what is only one reading as the only one that is possible. (Email communication, August 18, 2011).

Packer's words nicely summarize much of what I have been trying to say in this book, and they cut across the many different paradigms in qualitative inquiry and approaches to interviewing that I have addressed. Regardless of one's perspective, it is important to pay attention to the role of the social practice of interviewing in producing *what* is said, and *how* it is said in an interview, including awareness of the positionings of interviewer and interviewee. It is also important to focus on the pragmatics of speech—what the speaker is trying to accomplish through talk—in projects that are concerned with analyzing experiences of past events rather than analyzing conversation per se. The *how* of language and interaction is significant in constituting the *what* of what is said. Finally, remaining open for multiple readings and interpretations is a sign of quality, whereas attempts to close down alternative interpretations often betray the rich, varied, and open-ended nature of our conversational reality.

When reviewing manuscripts for qualitative journals, or dissertations based on qualitative research, I try to always think of the many kinds of virtues that may characterize a good research text. These can be ordered according to the ancient tripartite structure, going back at least to Plato, of the true, the good, and the beautiful. A good manuscript is—with the risk of sounding overly lofty—true, good, and beautiful. Few manuscripts excel in all three dimensions, and it may be enough to live up to the virtues of one or two of them. But they are in principle all relevant. Let me say a little bit about each in turn, conceiving these sets of criteria in terms of virtues. I call them epistemic, ethical, and aesthetic virtues, respectively (they were originally articulated in Brinkmann, 2012a, and are here expanded significantly).

As a caveat, however, I would like to emphasize my conviction that whenever we talk about quality criteria—whether they are epistemic, ethical, or aesthetic—we should bear in mind the pragmatic point that criteria are not universal, but are more like syndromes, without necessary and sufficient conditions. In Richard Rorty's words, criteria are "temporary resting places constructed for specific utilitarian ends." A criterion is what it is "because some social practice needs to block the road of inquiry, halt the regress of interpretations, in order to get something done" (Rorty, 1982, p. xli). If we have criteria, we should think of them as instruments that serve to improve our practices—not the other way round (develop practices that live up to criteria).

Epistemic Virtues

In light of the postmodern philosophies, which are very influential in qualitative inquiry (and some of which I have great sympathies for), it may sound strange to invoke a word like truth to describe good qualitative inquiry. I believe, however, that we still need this concept, perhaps not in an elevated metaphysical sense (Truth with a capital T), but in a more mundane sense (with a lower-case t), where it makes sense to draw a distinction between true and false accounts. As qualitative interviewers, for example, we want to remain true to what the participants have told us. We strive for what Alain Badiou (1998) has called "fidelity to the event" (see Parker, 2005, for an interpretation of this idea in relation to qualitative research). That something is true in this sense does not mean that it is true from a view from nowhere (Nagel, 1986), but it does mean that we have uncovered something from somewhere. Truth and relativity are thus not opposed. An example may illustrate this (from Burke, 1994, pp. 57–58): If I am driving on the highway and the car next to me is moving at a speed of 0 mph. relative to me, then this is an objectively true fact, even if I cannot say anything about how fast the car is moving according to a fixed (Newtonian) framework. As finite creatures, we can get truth from somewhere, but not from nowhere. Similarly, in qualitative interviewing, we have truths from somewhere, viz. from relationships and conversations with interviewees.

Let me add that it is not a province of research and science alone to get truth in this sense. In his famous essay on the origin of a work of art, Heidegger argued that for a work of art to be great, it has to be *true*. As he wrote: "In the artwork, the truth of beings has set itself to work. Art is truth setting itself to work." (Heidegger, 1993, p. 165). So for Heidegger, truth is not confined to science or logic, but can be an aspect of anything that conveys an experience of the truth of Being (as he would say). Truth in Heidegger's sense means that beings are brought into unconcealedness (*aletheia* in Greek). This is not truth as correct representation of the world, but truth as an *occurrence*, as something that happens (for example *as* a work of art). A work of art "is not the reproduction of some particular entity that happens to be at hand at any given time; it is, on the contrary, the reproduction of things' general essence." (p. 162). This, I would add, could also be a description of *true qualitative inquiry*.

Heidegger illustrates his point with a detailed analysis of van Gogh's painting of a pair of peasant shoes that point to the truth that "this equipment belongs to the *earth*" in Heidegger's special terminology (Heidegger, 1993, p. 159). According to more contemporary terminology that I have employed earlier in this book, we could say that Heidegger's notion of truth is connected to *showing* rather than *telling*. You can tell people many things that might be factually correct (e.g. that women are more prone to anxiety than men), but there are many things that can only be *shown* as truths (e.g. what the experience of anxiety feels like).

Qualitative analyses of interview materials can be true in a pragmatic, everyday sense, when they are *honest*, when the researcher *specifies her theoretical perspective*, when she *situates the participants, their statements, and episodes* that she addresses, when she *gives examples that back up her conclusions*, when she offers *a coherent account* of that which can be represented coherently—and offers fragments of that which is fragmented—and when she *creates a story that resonates in the reader* (Elliott, Fischer & Rennie, 1999). These are all epistemic criteria that remain signs of quality in qualitative interview studies, I believe, even after postmodernism.

Ethical Virtues

With the second set of criteria we are delving into difficult waters, for if people have a hard time agreeing on epistemic virtues, they often have even greater problems in agreeing on ethics—agreeing, for example, on what characterizes good research in an *ethical* sense. Even so, it seems to me evident that ethical virtues are inherent signs of quality in interview reports. Some qualitative researchers will even go so far as to argue that ethical criteria are the only important ones, leaving behind traditional scientific criteria of validity, reliability, and generalizability. A "methodology of the heart," for example, based on love, care, hope, and forgiveness has recently been advocated in this regard (Denzin, Lincoln & Giardina, 2006, p. 770). Subsuming qualitative inquiry entirely under the banner of ethics is a highly contested move (see Hammersley, 2008, for critical discussions), and my own view is that ethical virtues are *among* the ones to consider, but not the only relevant ones.

The emphasis on ethical virtues in the human and social sciences goes back as far as to Aristotle. As he stated in his *Ethics*, the political sciences (or what we would call the social sciences today), are species of *phronesis* or practical wisdom (Aristotle, 1976, p. 213), because they deal with human conduct as a highly particularistic, versatile, and changing phenomenon. Aristotle believed that practical knowledge about such things always "involves knowledge of particular facts, which become known from experience" (p. 215). We *know* about the social world (which is the goal of the social sciences), when we are able to *act well* as participants in our communities. *Knowing* well about human beings cannot on this account be separated from *acting* well among them. This line of thinking also fuelled American pragmatism in the 19th and 20th centuries, with people like Dewey and Rorty arguing that sciences are problem-solving tools that should be evaluated not in terms of Truth, but in terms of their contributions to human flourishing, the development of communities and democracies (see e.g. Brinkmann, 2004).

In recent years there has been a resurgence of interest in the Aristotelian view of the social sciences. To take an example that I have referred to a number of times, Robert Bellah and colleagues have developed what they call "social science as public philosophy" (Bellah, Madsen, Sullivan, Swidler & Tipton, 1985). This perspective accentuates the fact that the social researcher is within the society she is studying, and also within one or more of its moral traditions (p. 303). For qualitative interview research, this means that we should think of the researcher as a participant in social life, and as someone who addresses human lives and experiences through conversations. Social science as public philosophy is public in the sense that it is part of the ongoing discussion of the meaning and value of our common life, and as such it ideally engages the public.

Bent Flyvbjerg has argued quite specifically that the social sciences are—or must become, if they want to matter—*phronetic* (Flyvbjerg, 2001; this was discussed in Chapter 2 in relation to the ethics of research designs). According to Flyvbjerg, *phronetic* researchers place themselves within the context being studied and attempt to use the knowledge-producing capabilities of the human and social sciences to further discussions of the values of communities. This is done by asking three "value-rational" questions: Where are we going? Is this desirable? What should be done? (p. 60). The human and social sciences exist in practical webs of interpretation, and cannot for that reason produce "ideal theory," i.e., theory (as in physics) that transcends the vagaries of history and culture. But these sciences can instead assist in improving human practices.

In line with Flyvbjerg, the influential philosopher Charles Taylor has argued that social theory should be understood as a kind of social *practice*, with all the norms and values implied by this (Taylor, 1985). It is a practice that serves to interpret and articulate the meanings of human activity, but these articulations may enter people's self-understandings, thereby changing the realities they are concerned with. Taylor's point is that validity in the social sciences cannot mean mirroring some independent objects researched, because the objects of human and social science are *not* independent of human understanding (but are exactly *constituted* by such understanding). Thus, validity in the social sciences means *improving* the practices under consideration, and this is a moral issue. New interpretations can alter the self-understandings of those they describe, and social theories can thus be tested by examining the quality of the practices they inform and encourage (see also Brinkmann, 2011).

Judging a qualitative interview study in terms of its ethical virtues will in short mean that one is looking for its ability to *transform practice* in a fruitful direction, its *respect* for participants, which also means not seeking to transform them in a direction that they have not asked for, its sensitivity to issues of *confidentiality* and *consent*, its *faithfulness* to the lives and experiences of those portrayed, and its awareness of *power*, including the power of the interview to lure people into saying things that they would normally not be saying to strangers. There are, as Brinkmann and Kvale have argued, both micro ethical issues to consider in qualitative interviewing, having to do with the concrete relationships with participants and not harming them, and macro ethical issues about power-knowledge relationships in a societal context: Who is one doing research *for*? Who wins and who loses upon the publications of one's results? (Brinkmann & Kvale, 2005).

Aesthetic Virtues

Finally, as I have also touched upon a number of times in the previous chapters, aesthetic virtues are intrinsic to a good qualitative interview study. When a study works well aesthetically, aesthetics does not cloud what the researcher is trying to say, but makes the saying more precise, moving, evocative, and, in a paradoxical way perhaps, objective (Freeman, 2012). For aesthetics is not mere icing on a cake of science. The word comes from the Greek term for experience—that which we in fact sense—so when the goal of science is to convey human experience as precisely and as nuanced as possible, aesthetics is a tool rather than a hindrance. Pelias explains this poetically: "Science is the act of looking at a tree and seeing lumber. Poetry is the act of looking at a tree and seeing a tree." (Pelias, 2004, p. 9). If we want to understand trees rather than lumber, poetry, as an aesthetic practice, can be as precise (and, again, *objective*) as science. The poet, therefore, might in certain cases really be the one who can see the world clearly as it is, whereas "scientific" perspectives risk reducing the phenomena to something else, or instrumentalizing them.

Qualitative researchers such as Richardson (Richardson & Lockridge, 1998) and Bochner (2002) have stressed the aesthetic dimension as perhaps the most important one in qualitative inquiry. For the reader has to be *moved* by what she reads, if the text is going to make a difference. In Chapter 4, I summarized Bochner's list of aesthetic virtues, which includes the reporting of many concrete details (incorporating the researcher's own feelings and doubts), the inclusion of structurally complex narratives that are communicated with honesty, credibility, and vulnerability in a way that relates to some process of human development, and which is based on ethical self-consciousness.

With this list, we are perhaps witnessing an (almost Platonic) reintegration of the true, the good, and the beautiful, as it becomes difficult to distinguish the aesthetic virtues from the other ones. This is as it should be, I believe, for it reminds us that the point is not necessarily to turn qualitative interviewers into artists. Arts-based research is a very welcome approach in qualitative inquiry (Leavy, 2009), but not all qualitative research is art. All high-quality qualitative research does, however, have aesthetic qualities that are shared with the arts, and the point is that these qualities are often what enable readers to understand the phenomena described by the researcher.

So the point is simply that interview researchers should think more about the aesthetics of their reports. Writing is a craft and arguably the single most important practice of qualitative researchers, and given its centrality in the research process, it is surprising how little attention writing is given in most departments, programs, and courses in qualitative research. One of the purposes of this book is to enable qualitative interviewers to craft better research reports, and to enable readers of such reports to ask relevant questions to the products of the craftsmanship. The point is not to choose between epistemic, ethical, and aesthetic virtues when doing and evaluating research based on qualitative interviewing, but to be clear about which criteria one invokes and why. I personally like to think that all sets of criteria are (almost) always relevant.

REFERENCES AND RESOURCES

Before the list of references used in this book, I have singled out a number of significant books of qualitative interviewing to form a list of suggested readings. Some are empirical studies, while others are important methodological texts.

Suggested readings

Adorno, T.W., Frenkel-Brunswik, E., Levinson, D.J. & Sanford, R.N. (1950). *The Authoritarian Personality*. New York: Norton.
Published in 1950, following the end of World War II, this book used interviews along with other approaches such as psychometrics to understand the authoritarian personality, which, according to the researchers, led to prejudice and fascism. The book has been strongly criticized, but remains essential in sociology, psychology, and political science.
Bellah, R.N., Madsen, R., Sullivan, W.M., Swidler, A. & Tipton, S.M. (1985). *Habits of the Heart: Individualism and Commitment in American Life*. Berkeley: University of California Press.
This book reports the results of a large interview study concerned with North American character and values. It nicely weaves together empirical and philosophical issues, and succeeded in generating public discussion about significant societal issues of individualism.
Fontana, A. & Prokos, A.H. (2007). *The Interview: From Formal to Postmodern*. Walnut Creek, CA: Left Coast Press.
This short book provides an introduction to many different varieties of interviewing, notably of more postmodern kinds.
Holstein, J.A. & Gubrium, J.F. (1995). *The Active Interview*. London: Sage.

Holstein and Gubrium's slim volume has become a methodological classic because of its fresh approach to qualitative interviewing, which emphasized the active role of the interviewer as a co-constructor of knowledge.

Kinsey, A.C., Pomeroy, W.B. & Martin, C.E. (1948). *Sexual Behavior in the Human Male*. Philadelphia: Saunders.

The book by Kinsey and coworkers has been singled out as dangerous by conservative critics, but it is undoubtedly one of the most influential interview studies ever reported. It has assisted in changing our conceptions of sexuality and is proof that interview studies can have a huge cultural impact.

Kvale, S. & Brinkmann, S. (2008). *InterViews: Learning the Craft of Qualitative Research Interviewing*. (2nd ed.). Thousand Oaks, CA: Sage.

Steinar Kvale was a pioneer in qualitative interview research, and this book—now in its second edition—takes the reader through all stages of interviewing and has a particular focus on how to interview well for research purposes.

Lather, P. & Smithies, C. (1997). *Troubling the Angels*. Boulder, CO: Westview Press.

Beautifully written, evocative, and experimental, the Lather and Smithies book about women living with HIV/AIDS demonstrates how postmodern ways of doing and reporting interview studies can be of very high quality.

Mishler, E. (1986). *Research Interviewing—Context and Narrative*. Cambridge, MA: Harvard University Press.

Mishler's book on qualitative interviewing is theoretically rich and zooms in on interviewing as a joint production of meaning.

Murakami, H. (2003). *Underground: The Tokyo Gas Attack and the Japanese Psyche*. London: Vintage Books.

I have celebrated Murakami's book already on the preceding pages, and it is worth reading for everyone who would like to see an example of a culturally relevant, thorough, and extremely well-written interview study—in spite of (or because of?) the author's background as a novelist.

Roulston, K. (2010). *Reflective Interviewing: A Guide to Theory and Practice*. Thousand Oaks, CA: Sage.

This book gives a theoretical introduction to many different forms of qualitative interviewing, and is also rich in empirical examples and details.

Rubin, H.J. & Rubin, I.S. (2012). *Qualitative Interviewing: The Art of Hearing Data*. (Third edition). Thousand Oaks, CA: Sage.

The Rubin and Rubin text is a classic introduction to responsive interviewing, i.e. to one specific kind of qualitative interviewing that is empathetic and receptive.

Silvester, E. (1993). *The Penguin Book of Interviews*. London: Penguin.

This is a collection of interviews from many different sources. They are not as such qualitative research interviews, but the qualitative interviewer may still learn a lot from reading the interviews with famous people from different historical periods.

Spradley, J. (1979). *The Ethnographic Interview*. New York: Holt, Rinehart & Winston.

Conceiving of interviewing as part of ethnographic fieldwork, Spradley's book is full of useful advice for the novice interviewer about how to ask questions and follow up.

Wengraf, T. (2001). *Qualitative Research Interviewing.* Thousand Oaks, CA: Sage.

For people who are interested in biographic narrative interviewing, Wengraf's book is an indispensable resource that treats this particular approach to interviewing in great detail—both theoretically and practically.

References

Adorno, T.W., Frenkel-Brunswik, E., Levinson, D.J. & Sanford, R.N. (1950). *The Authoritarian Personality.* New York: Norton.

Alvesson, M. & Kärreman, D. (2011). *Qualitative Research and Theory Development: Mystery as Method.* London: Sage.

Aristotle (1976). *Nichomachean Ethics.* London: Penguin.

Atkinson, P. (2002). The life story interview. In J.F. Gubrium & J.A. Holstein (Eds.), *Handbook of Interview Research: Context & Method* (pp. 121–140). Thousand Oaks, CA: Sage.

Atkinson, P. & Silverman, D. (1997). Kundera's Immortality: The Interview Society and the Invention of the Self. *Qualitative Inquiry, 3,* 304–325.

Badiou, A. (1998). *Ethics: An Essay on the Understanding of Evil.* London: Verso.

Bellah, R.N., Madsen, R., Sullivan, W.M., Swidler, A. & Tipton, S.M. (1985). *Habits of the Heart: Individualism and Commitment in American Life.* Berkeley: University of California Press.

Bernstein, R.J. (2010). *The Pragmatic Turn.* Cambridge: Polity Press.

Billig, M. (1999). *Freudian Repression: Conversation Creating the Unconscious.* Cambridge: Cambridge University Press.

Blumer, H. (1969). *Symbolic Interactionism: Perspective and Method.* Englewood Cliffs, NJ: Prentice-Hall.

Bochner, A.P. (2002). Criteria against ourselves. In N.K. Denzin & Y.S. Lincoln (Eds.), *The Qualitative Inquiry Reader* (pp. 257–265). Thousand Oaks, CA: Sage.

Bogardus, E.M. (1924). Methods of interviewing. *Journal of Applied Sociology, 9,* 456–467.

Briggs, C. (2003). Interviewing, power/knowledge, and social inequality. In J.A. Holstein & J.F. Gubrium (Eds.), *Inside Interviewing: New Lenses, New Concerns* (pp. 495–506). Thousand Oaks, CA: Sage.

Briggs, C. (2007). Anthropology, interviewing and communicability in contemporary society. *Current Anthropology, 48,* 551–567.

Brinkmann, S. (2004). Psychology as a Moral Science: Aspects of John Dewey's psychology. *History of the Human Sciences, 17,* 1–28.

Brinkmann, S. (2007a). Could interviews be epistemic? An alternative to qualitative opinion-polling. *Qualitative Inquiry, 13,* 1116–1138.

Brinkmann, S. (2007b). The good qualitative researcher. *Qualitative Research in Psychology, 4,* 127–144.

Brinkmann, S. (2011). *Psychology as a Moral Science: Perspectives on Normativity.* New York: Springer.

Brinkmann, S. (2012a). *Qualitative Inquiry in Everyday Life: Working with Everyday Life Materials.* London: Sage.

Brinkmann, S. (2012b). Qualitative research between craftsmanship and McDonaldization. *Qualitative Studies, 3*, 56–68.

Brinkmann, S. & Kvale, S. (2005). Confronting the Ethics of Qualitative Research. *Journal of Constructivist Psychology, 18*, 157–181.

Bruner, J. (1991). The Narrative Construction of Reality. *Critical Inquiry, 18*, 1–21.

Burke, T. (1994). *Dewey's New Logic: A Reply to Russell.* Chicago: University of Chicago Press.

Butler, J. (2005). *Giving an Account of Oneself.* New York: Fordham University Press.

Charmaz, K. (1999). Stories of suffering: Subjective tales and research narratives. *Qualitative Health Research, 9*, 362–382.

Charmaz, K. (2011). Grounded theory methods in social justice research. In N.K. Denzin & Y.S. Lincoln (Eds.), *The SAGE Handbook of Qualitative Research* (pp. 359–380). Thousand Oaks, CA: Sage.

Chrzanowska, J. (2002). *Interviewing Groups and Individuals in Qualitative Market Research.* Thousand Oaks, CA: Sage.

Clarke, A. (2005). *Situational Analysis: Grounded Theory After the Postmodern Turn.* Thousand Oaks, CA: Sage.

Clifford, J. & Marcus, G. (1986). *Writing Culture: The Poetics and Politics of Ethnography.* Berkeley, CA: The University of California Press.

Conrad, R.G. & Schober, M. (2008). New frontiers in standardized survey interviewing. In S.N. Hesse-Biber & P. Leavy (Eds.), *Handbook of Emergent Methods* (pp. 173–188). London: The Guilford Press.

Dahler-Larsen, P. (2008). *Displaying Qualitative Data.* Odense: University Press of Southern Denmark.

Denzin, N.K. (1997). *Interpretive Ethnography: Ethnographic Practices for the 21st Century.* Thousand Oaks, CA: Sage.

Denzin, N.K. (2001). *Interpretive Interactionism.* (2nd ed.). Thousand Oaks, CA: Sage.

Denzin, N.K., Lincoln, Y.S. & Giardina, M. (2006). Disciplining qualitative research. *International Journal of Qualitative Studies in Education, 19*, 769–782.

Dichter, E. (1960). *The Strategy of Desire.* Garden City, NY: Doubleday.

Dinkins, C.S. (2005). Shared Inquiry: Socratic-Hermeneutic Interpre-viewing. In P. Ironside (Ed.), *Beyond Method: Philosophical Conversations in Healthcare Research and Scholarship* (pp. 111–147). Madison, WI: University of Wisconsin Press.

Edwards, D. (2004). Analyzing racial discourse: The discursive psychology of mind-world relationships. In H. van den Berg & M. Wetherell (Eds.), *Analyzing Race Talk: Multidisciplinary Perspectives on the Research Interview* (pp. 31–48). Cambridge: Cambridge University Press.

Elliott, K., Fischer, C.T. & Rennie, D.L. (1999). Evolving guidelines for publication of qualitative research studies in psychology and related fields. *British Journal of Clinical Psychology, 38*, 215–229.

Ellis, C., Adams, T.E. & Bochner, A.P. (2011). Autoethography: An overview. *Forum: Qualitative Social Research, 12*, Article 10-http://www.qualitative-research.net/index.php/fqs/article/viewArticle/1589/3095.

Ellis, C. & Berger, L. (2003). Their story/my story/our story: Including the researcher's experience in interview research. In J.A. Holstein & J.F. Gubrium (Eds.), *Inside Interviewing: New Lenses, New Concerns* (pp. 467–493). Thousand Oaks, CA: Sage.

Flick, U. (2002). *An Introduction to Qualitative Research*. (2nd edition). London: Sage.

Flyvbjerg, B. (2001). *Making Social Science Matter—Why social inquiry fails and how it can succeed again*. Cambridge: Cambridge University Press.

Flyvbjerg, B. (2006). Five misunderstandings about case-study research. *Qualitative Inquiry, 12*, 219–245.

Fontana, A. & Prokos, A.H. (2007). *The Interview: From Formal to Postmodern*. Walnut Creek, CA: Left Coast Press.

Freeman, M. (2012). Qualitative inquiry and the self-realization of psychological science. *Qualitative Inquiry, In press,*

Freud, S. (1963). *Therapy and Technique*. New York: Collier.

Frosh, S. (2007). Disintegrating qualitative research. *Theory & Psychology, 17*, 635–653.

Gadamer, H.G. (1960). *Truth and Method*. (Second revised edition published 2000). New York: Continuum.

Garfinkel, H. (1967). *Studies in Ethnomethodology*. (This edition 1984). Cambridge: Polity Press.

Geertz, C. (1973). *The Interpretation of Cultures*. New York: Basic Books.

Gergen, K.J. (2001). *Social Construction in Context*. London: Sage.

Gibbs, G. (2007). *Analyzing Qualitative Data*. London: Sage.

Giorgi, A. & Giorgi, B. (2003). The Descriptive Phenomenological Psychological Method. In P.M. Camic, J.E. Rhodes, & L. Yardley (Eds.), *Qualitative Research in Psychology: Expanding Perspectives in Methodology and Design* (pp. 243–273). Washington, DC: American Psychological Association.

Glaser, B.G. & Strauss, A. (1967). *The Discovery of Grounded Theory: Strategies for Qualitative Research*. New York: Aldine Publishing Company.

Hammersley, M. (2008). *Questioning Qualitative Inquiry: Critical Essays*. London: Sage.

Hammersley, M. (2011). *Methodology: Who Needs It?* London: Sage.

Hansen, D.L. & Hansen, E.H. (2006). Caught in a balancing act: Parents' dilemmas regarding their ADHD child's treatment with stimulant medication. *Qualitative Health Research, 16*, 1267–1285.

Harré, R. (1983). *Personal Being*. Oxford: Basil Blackwell.

Harré, R. (2004). Staking our claim for qualitative psychology as science. *Qualitative Research in Psychology, 1*, 3–14.

Harrington, W. (1997). A writer's essay: Seeking the extraordinary in the ordinary. In W. Harrington (Ed.), *Intimate Journalism: The Art and Craft of Reporting Everyday Life* (pp. xvii–xlvi). Thousand Oaks, CA: Sage.

Heidegger, M. (1993). The origin of the work of art. In D.F. Krell (Ed.), *Martin Heidegger: Basic Writings* (pp. 143–212). London: Routledge.

Hollway, W. & Jefferson, T. (2000). Biography, Anxiety and the Experience of Locality. In P. Chamberlayne, J. Bornat, & T. Wengraf (Eds.), *The Turn to Biographical Methods in Social Science* (pp. 167–180). London: Routledge.

Holstein, J.A. & Gubrium, J.F. (1995). *The Active Interview*. London: Sage.

Husserl, E. (1954). *Die Krisis der europäischen Wissenschaften und die tranzendentale Phänomenologie*. Haag: Martinus Nijhoff.

Ingold, T. (2011). *Being Alive: Essays on Movement, Knowledge and Description*. London: Routledge.

Jefferson, G. (1985). An exercise in the transcription and analysis of laughter. In T. Van Dijk (Ed.), *Handbook of Discourse Analysis, Volume 3* (pp. 25–34). London: Academic Press.

Kawamura, S. (1959). The process of sub-culture propagation among Japanese macaques. *Primates, 2,* 43–60.

Kinsey, A.C., Pomeroy, W.B. & Martin, C.E. (1948). *Sexual Behavior in the Human Male*. Philadelphia: Saunders.

Kohlberg, L. (1981). *Essays on Moral Development Volume 1—The Philosophy of Moral Development*. San Fransisco: Harper & Row Publishers.

Kuhn, T.S. (1970). *The Structure of Scientific Revolutions*. (Second enlarged edition). Chicago: University of Chicago Press.

Kvale, S. (1980). *Spillet om karakterer i gymnasiet: Elevinterviews om bivirkninger af adgangsbegrænsning*. Copenhagen: Munksgaard.

Kvale, S. (1996). *InterViews: An Introduction to Qualitative Research Interviewing*. Thousand Oaks, CA: Sage.

Kvale, S. (2003). The psychoanalytical interview as inspiration for qualitative research. In P.M. Camic & J.E. Rhodes (Eds.), *Qualitative research in psychology: Expanding perspectives in methodology and design* (pp. 275–297). Washington, DC, US: American Psychological Association.

Kvale, S. (2008). Qualitative inquiry between scientistic evidentialism, ethical subjectivism and the free market. *International Review of Qualitative Research, 1,* 5–18.

Kvale, S. & Brinkmann, S. (2008). *InterViews: Learning the Craft of Qualitative Research Interviewing*. (2nd ed.). Thousand Oaks, CA: Sage.

Langdridge, D. (2007). *Phenomenological Psychology: Theory, Research and Method*. Harlow: Pearson Education.

Lather, P. & Smithies, C. (1997). *Troubling the Angels*. Boulder, CO: Westview Press.

Latour, B. (1997). Foreword: Stengers's Shibboleth. In I. Stengers (Ed.), *Power and Invention* (pp. vii–xx). Minneapolis: University of Minnesota Press.

Latour, B. (2000). When things strike back: a possible contribution of "science studies" to the social sciences. *British Journal of Sociology, 50,* 107–123.

Lave, J. (1988). *Cognition in Practice: Mind, Mathematics and Culture in Everyday Life*. Cambridge: Cambridge University Press.

Lave, J. & Kvale, S. (1995). What is anthropological research? An interview with Jean Lave by Steinar Kvale. *Qualitative Studies in Education, 8,* 219–228.

Leavy, P. (2009). *Method Meets Art: Arts-Based Research Practice*. New York: Guilford Press.

Leavy, P. (2011). *Oral History*. Oxford: Oxford University Press.

Lee, R.M. (2008). David Riesman and the sociology of the interview. *The Sociological Quarterly, 49,* 285–307.

Lee, R.M. (2011). "The most important technique…": Carl Rogers, Hawthorne, and the rise and fall of nondirective interviewing in sociology. *Journal of the History of the Behavioral Sciences, 47,* 123–146.

Levinas, E. (1969). *Totality and Infinity: An Essay on Exteriority.* Pittsburgh: Duquesne University Press.

Lyotard, J.-F. (1984). *The Postmodern Condition: A Report on Knowledge.* Manchester: Manchester University Press.

Maccoby, E.E. & Maccoby, N. (1954). The interview: A tool of social science. In G. Lindzey (Ed.), *Handbook of Social Psychology* (pp. 449–487). Cambridge, MA: Addison-Wesley.

Mann, C. & Stewart, F. (2002). Internet interviewing. In J.F. Gubrium & J.A. Holstein (Eds.), *Handbook of Interview Research: Context & Method* (pp. 603–627). Thousand Oaks, CA: Sage.

Mannheim, B. & Tedlock, B. (1995). Introduction. In B. Tedlock & B. Mannheim (Eds.), *The Dialogic Emergence of Culture* (pp. 1–31). Urbana, IL: University of Illinois Press.

Markham, A. (2005). The methods, politics, and ethics of representation in online ethnography. In N.K. Denzin & Y.S. Lincoln (Eds.), *The SAGE Handbook of Qualitative Research.* (3rd edition) (pp. 247–283). Thousand Oaks, CA: Sage.

Marshall, C. & Rossman, G.B. (2006). *Designing Qualitative Research.* Thousand Oaks, CA: Sage.

Mayo, E. (1933). *The Social Problems of an Industrial Civilization.* New York: MacMillan.

Merleau-Ponty, M. (1945). *Phenomenology of Perception.* (This edition published 2002). London: Routledge.

Mills, C.W. (1959). *The Sociological Imagination.* (This edition 2000). Oxford: Oxford University Press.

Mishler, E. (1986). *Research Interviewing—Context and Narrative.* Cambridge, MA: Harvard University Press.

Morgan, D.L. (2002). Focus group interviewing. In J.F. Gubrium & J.A. Holstein (Eds.), *Handbook of Interview Research: Context & Method* (pp. 141–161). Thousand Oaks, CA: Sage.

Morse, J. (2006). The politics of evidence. In N.K. Denzin & M. Giardina (Eds.), *Qualitative Inquiry and the Conservative Challenge* (pp. 79–92). Walnut Creek, CA: Left Coast Press.

Morse, J. & Mitcham, C. (1998). The experience of agonizing pain and signals of disembodiment. *Journal of Psychosomatic Research, 44,* 667–680.

Morse, J., Niehaus, L., Wolfe, R.R. & Wilkins, S. (2006). The role of the theoretical drive in maintaining validity in mixed-methods research. *Qualitative Research in Psychology, 3,* 279–291.

Mulhall, S. (2007). *The Conversation of Humanity.* Charlottesville: University of Virginia Press.

Murakami, H. (2003). *Underground: The Tokyo Gas Attack and the Japanese Psyche.* London: Vintage Books.

Musaeus, P. & Brinkmann, S. (2011). The semiosis of family conflict: A case study of home-based psychotherapy. *Culture & Psychology, 17,* 47–63.

Nagel, T. (1986). *The View from Nowhere.* Oxford: Oxford University Press.

Noblit, G.W. & Hare, R.D. (1988). *Meta-Ethnography: Synthesizing Qualitative Studies.* Newbury Park, CA: Sage.

Packer, M. (2011). *The Science of Qualitative Research*. Cambridge: Cambridge University Press.

Parker, I. (2004). Criteria for qualitative research in psychology. *Qualitative Research in Psychology, 1*, 95–106.

Parker, I. (2005). *Qualitative Psychology: Introducing Radical Research*. Buckingham: Open University Press.

Pascale, C.-M. (2011). *Cartographies of Knowledge: Exploring Qualitative Epistemologies*. Thousand Oaks, CA: Sage.

Pavlenko, A. (2007). Autobiographic narratives as data in applied linguistics. *Applied Linguistics, 28*, 163–188.

Pelias, R. (2004). *A Methodology of the Heart: Evoking Academic and Daily Life*. Walnut Creek, CA: AltaMira Press.

Piaget, J. (1930). *The Child's Conception of the World*. New York: Harcourt, Brace & World.

Piaget, J. (1932). *The Moral Judgment of the Child*. (This edition published 1975). London: Routledge & Kegan Paul.

Plato (1987). *The Republic*. London: Penguin.

Platt, J. (2002). The history of the interview. In J.F. Gubrium & J.A. Holstein (Eds.), *Handbook of Interview Research: Context and Method* (pp. 33–54). Thousand Oaks, CA: Sage.

Pollio, H.R., Henley, T.B. & Thompson, C.J. (1997). *The Phenomenology of Everyday Life*. Cambridge: Cambridge University Press.

Potter, J. & Hepburn, A. (2005). Qualitative interviews in psychology: Problems and possibilities. *Qualitative Research in Psychology, 2*, 281–307.

Potter, J. & Wetherell, M. (1987). *Discourse and Social Psychology*. London: Sage.

Rapley, T.J. (2001). The art(fulness) of open-ended interviewing: Some considerations on analysing interviews. *Qualitative Research, 1*, 303–323.

Reinharz, S. & Chase, S.E. (2002). Interviewing women. In J.F. Gubrium & J.A. Holstein (Eds.), *Handbook of Interview Research: Context & Method* (pp. 221–238). Thousand Oaks, CA: Sage.

Richardson, L. & Lockridge, E. (1998). Fiction and Ethnography: A Conversation. *Qualitative Inquiry, 4*, 328–336.

Richardson, L. & St.Pierre, E.A. (2005). Writing: A method of inquiry. In N.K. Denzin & Y.S. Lincoln (Eds.), *Handbook of Qualitative Research*. (3rd edition) (pp. 959–978). Thousand Oaks, CA: Sage.

Riesman, D.M. & Benney, M. (1956). The sociology of the interview. *Midwestern Sociologist, 18*, 3–15.

Roethlishberger, F.J. & Dickson, W.J. (1939). *Management and the Worker*. New York: Wiley.

Rogers, C. (1945). The Non-directive Method as a Technique for Social Research. *The American Journal of Sociology, 50*, 279–283.

Rorty, R. (1982). *Consequences of Pragmatism*. Brighton: Harvester.

Roulston, K. (2010). *Reflective Interviewing: A Guide to Theory and Practice*. Thousand Oaks, CA: Sage.

Roulston, K. (2011). Interview "problems" as topics for analysis. *Applied Linguistics, 32*, 77–94.

Rubin, H.J. & Rubin, I.S. (2012). *Qualitative Interviewing: The Art of Hearing Data*. (Third edition). Thousand Oaks, CA: Sage.

Ryen, A. (2002). Cross-cultural interviewing. In J.F. Gubrium & J.A. Holstein (Eds.), *Handbook of Interview Research: Context & Method* (pp. 335–354). Thousand Oaks, CA: Sage.

Sarbin, T.R. (1986). The narrative as a root metaphor for psychology. In T.R. Sarbin (Ed.), *Narrative Psychology: The Storied Nature of Human Conduct* (pp. 3–21). New York: Praeger.

Scott, S. (2009). *Making Sense of Everyday Life*. Cambridge: Polity Press.

Shotter, J. (1993). *Conversational Realities: Constructing Life through Language*. London: Sage.

Shuy, R.W. (2002). In-person versus telephone interviewing. In J.F. Gubrium & J.A. Holstein (Eds.), *Handbook of Interview Research: Context & Method* (pp. 537–556). Thousand Oaks, CA: Sage.

Shweder, R.A. & Much, N. (1987). Determinations of meaning: Discourse and moral socialization. In W.M. Kurtines & J.L. Gewirtz (Eds.), *Moral Development Through Social Interaction* (pp. 197–244). New York: Wiley.

Silverman, D. (2000). *Doing Qualitative Research: A Practical Handbook*. London: Sage.

Silvester, E. (1993). *The Penguin Book of Interviews*. London: Penguin.

Skårderud, F. (2003). Sh@me in cyberspace. Relationships without faces: The e-media and eating disorders. *European Eating Disorders Review, 11*, 155–169.

Smith, L.T. (1999). *Decolonizing Methodologies: Research and Indigeneous People*. London: Zed Books.

Sorsoli, L. & Tolman, D.L. (2008). Hearing voices: Listening for multiplicity and movement in interview data. In S.N. Hesse-Biber & P. Leavy (Eds.), *Handbook of Emergent Methods* (pp. 495–515). London: The Guilford Press.

Spradley, J. (1979). *The Ethnographic Interview*. New York: Holt, Rinehart & Winston.

Strauss, A. & Corbin, J. (1990). *Basics of Qualitative Research*. Newbury Park, CA: Sage.

Talmy, S. (2010). Qualitative interviews in applied linguistics: From research instrument to social practice. *Annual Review of Applied Linguistics, 30*, 128–148.

Tanggaard, L. (2007). The Research Interview as Discourses Crossing Swords. *Qualitative Inquiry, 13*, 160–176.

Taylor, C. (1985). Social Theory as Practice. In *Philosophy and the Human Sciences: Philosophical Papers 2* (pp. 91–115). Cambridge: Cambridge University Press.

Taylor, C. (1989). *Sources of the Self*. Cambridge: Cambridge University Press.

Thomsen, D.K. & Brinkmann, S. (2009). An interviewer's guide to autobiographical memory: Ways to elicit concrete experiences and to avoid pitfalls in interpreting them. *Qualitative Research in Psychology, 6*, 294–312.

Trevarthen, C. (1993). The self born in intersubjectivity: The psychology of an infant communicating. In U. Neisser (Ed.), *The Perceived Self* (pp. 121–173). Cambridge: Cambridge University Press.

Valsiner, J. (2007). *Culture in minds and societies: Foundations of cultural psychology*. New Delhi: Sage.

Van Maanen, J. (1988). *Tales of the Field*. Chicago: University of Chicago Press.

Wacquant, L. (1995). The pugilistic point of view: How boxers think and feel about their trade. *Theory & Society, 24*, 489–535.

Warren, C.A.B. (2002). Qualitative interviewing. In J.F. Gubrium & J.A. Holstein (Eds.), *Handbook of Interview Research: Context & Method* (pp. 83–101). Thousand Oaks, CA: Sage.

Wengraf, T. (2001). *Qualitative Research Interviewing*. Thousand Oaks, CA: Sage.

Wolcott, H. (2009). *Writing Up Qualitative Research*. (3rd ed.). Thousand Oaks, CA: Sage.

Young, I.M. (1980). Throwing like a girl: A phenomenology of feminine body comportment, motility and spatiality. *Human Studies, 3*, 137–156.

INDEX

Note: Page numbers followed by italicized letters indicate text found in boxes (*b*), footnotes (*n*) and tables (*t*).

abduction/abductive reasoning, 55–56, 65–66, 118
abstract, in interview report, 86
The Active Interview (Holstein and Gubrium), 31
active interviewing, 32–34, 74
ADHD report, methods section example, 94–98
Adorno, T.W., 10
aesthetic virtues, 156–158
"allow the objects to object," 69
Alvesson, M., 118
analysis, of interviews
    coding, 62, 117
    models of, 53–56, 62–66, 117–118
    transcription, 61–62, 99
analytic approaches
    interviews as research instruments, 37–38
    interviews as social practice, 38–39
    phenomenological, 22–23, 36–38, 63–64

"analytic induction," 62
analytic story, 117, 138
anthropological method, 107
Aristotle, 155
art, as truth, 153
Ashok dilemma (Heinz dilemma), 34
assertive interview style, 31–32
asymmetrical distribution of talk, 17
Atkinson, P., 5
authenticity of data, 113–114
authoritarianism, study of, 10
The Authoritarian Personality (Adorno), 10

Badiou, Alain, 153
Bellah, R.N., 73, 80, 104, 108
Benney, Mark, 9–10
Billig, Michael, 7
biographical-narrative interviews, 20
"black swans," 65
Blumer, Herbert, 64
Bochner, A.P., 115–116, 157

receptive interview style, 31
reflexive objectivity, 108–109
report, common elements of
  conclusion, 93–94
  findings section, 91–93
  introduction, 85–87
  literature review, 87–89
  methods section, 89–91
  standard reports, 84–85
  reporting, of results, 66–67. *See also*
    writing, of research findings
The Republic (Plato), 32
research design
  analysis, 61–66
  construction model of, 67, 72–75
  discovery model of, 67–72
  interviewing, 59–61
  preparation
    areas of study, 47–48
    confidentiality in, 52
    control groups, 48–49
    design questions, 49
    how many interviews, 58–59
    how to study, 52–57
    informed consent in, 51–52
    literature review in, 51
    what should be studied, 49–50
    who should be interviewed, 57–58
    why (relevance of study), 50–52
  reporting, 66–67
  understanding model of, 67, 75–79
researcher reflexivity, 142–143
research instruments, interviews as, 37–38
Research Interviewing—Context and Narrative (Mishler), 11
resonance, with readers, 129*b*
response, variation in, 31–32
responsive interviewing, 60
Richardson, L., 103, 126–127, 157
Riesman, David, 9–10
Roethlisberger, F.J., 8
Rogers, Carl, 9, 12, 13, 31
romantic interview concepts, 12
Rorty, Richard, 152, 155
Rossman, G.B., 47

Roulston, K., 12, 17, 31, 57, 65

sampling/selection distinction, 57–58
scenes, writing in, 128*b*
Schober, M., 20
Schutz, Alfred, 95
The Science of Qualitative Research (Packer), 76, 151
scientific method, 141–142
Scott, S., 119
Seale, Clive, 37
selection/sampling distinction, 57–58
"self-transcribing" interviews, 30
semi-structured interviews
  defined, 21
  descriptions in, 22, 25
  interpretations in, 23–25
  life world concept in, 22–23
  purpose, 21
Sennett, Richard, 108
sensitizing instruments/concepts, 64, 65
Sexual Behavior in the Human Male (Kinsey), 10
sexuality, study of, 10
Shotter, John, 3
Shuy, R. W., 29
Shweder, R.A., 34
Silverman, D., 5, 86, 88, 89–90, 117
situated interaction
  data in, 92
  interviews as form of, 52, 66, 126
  in social practice, 37*t*, 39
  talk as, 131*b*
situational analysis, 63
Skårderud, Finn, 30
Smithies, Chris, 105
social practice, interviews as, 37*t*, 38–39
social reality, 23*n*2
social sciences
  concept of conversation in, 3
  as *phronetic*, 51, 155
  qualitative interviewing in, 36–42
social sciences interviews, emergence of, 1*n*, 3
society/culture, study of, 47–48

Lightning Source UK Ltd.
Milton Keynes UK
UKHW040645291118
333105UK00001B/20/P